Skills for First Certificate

Use of English

Malcolm Mann
Steve Taylore-Knowles

Macmillan Education
Between Towns Road, Oxford OX4 3PP
A division of Macmillan Publishers Limited
Companies and representatives throughout the world

ISBN 978 1 4050 1751 0

Text and design © Macmillan Publishers Limited 2003

First published 2003

All rights reserved; no part of this publication may be
reproduced, stored in a retrieval system, transmitted in
any form, or by any means, electronic, mechanical,
photocopying, recording, or otherwise, without the
prior permission of the publishers.

Designed by Marc Theriault at Polyplano, Thessaloniki, Greece
Design development by Thomas Nicolaou at Polyplano
Cover design by Marc Theriault
Series editor: Emma Parker

Cover image and text extracts from the *Macmillan English Dictionary*,
published by Macmillan Publishers Limited 2002
text © Bloomsbury Publishers Plc 2002

Malcolm Mann would like to thank everyone at Macmillan and Macmillan Zenith
for all their support and encouragement during the writing of this series.

Steve Taylore-Knowles would like to thank Jeanne, Sue, Emma, Yanni and George
for making it happen and keeping it fun, Malc for putting up with putting him up,
Jo for just putting up with him, and all his FC students whose faces and voices
were constantly in his mind as he wrote.

The publishers would like to thank Ann Gibson, ELT Consultant.

The authors and publishers would like to thank the following for permission to reproduce
their photographs: CORBIS Images (UK) pp6(Brandtner & Staedeli), 12(John Hulme;Eye
Ubiquitous(B), Patrick Giardino(C)), 15, 22(Catherine Karnow), 28(Chris Daniels),
38(Rune Hellestad), 44(Colin Garrat;Milepost 92), 54(Lynn Goldsmith), 60, 70(Joseph
Sohm;ChromoSohm Inc.), 76(John Wilkinson;Ecoscene(A), Michael S. Yamashita(B),
Sally A. Morgan;Ecoscene(C)), 86(Phil Schermeister), 92(Roger Ressmeyer(A), Keren
Su(B)), 94(Michael A. Keller Studios, Ltd), 102(Patricia McDonough), 108(Helen King),
118(Joseph Sohm;ChromoSohm, Inc.), 124(Roy Botterell), Digital Stock/Corbis 72.

Printed and bound in Thailand

2014 2013 2012
15   14   13

Contents

	Topic	Skills focus	Exam practice	Grammar focus	Page
1	Films	**Multiple choice cloze:** lexical collocations and items	Part 1	expressing present time	6
2	Occupations	**Open cloze:** lexico-grammatical collocations and patterns	Part 2	expressing past time	12
	Practice Exam 1				18
3	Education	**Key word transformations:** grammatical items	Part 3	linking present and past time	22
4	Sport	**Error correction:** lexical collocations and items	Part 4	expressing future time	28
	Practice Exam 2				34
5	People	**Word formation:** prefixes	Part 5	comparatives and superlatives	38
6	Travel	**Multiple choice cloze:** lexico-grammatical collocations and patterns	Part 1	modals I	44
	Practice Exam 3				50
7	Food and Drink	**Open cloze:** grammatical items	Part 2	modals II	54
8	The Media	**Key word transformations:** lexical collocations and items	Part 3	reported speech and reported questions	60
	Practice Exam 4				66
9	The Weather	**Error correction:** lexico-grammatical collocations and patterns	Part 4	relative clauses	70
10	The Environment	**Word formation:** suffixes	Part 5	result clauses	76
	Practice Exam 5				82
11	Technology	**Multiple choice cloze:** grammatical items	Part 1	conditionals	86
12	Health and Fitness	**Open cloze:** lexical collocations and items	Part 2	passive voice	92
	Practice Exam 6				98
13	Transport	**Key word transformations:** lexico-grammatical collocations and patterns	Part 3	causative form	102
14	Fashion	**Error correction:** grammatical items	Part 4	wishes	108
	Practice Exam 7				114
15	Crime	**Word formation:** irregular forms	Part 5	countable and uncountable nouns	118
16	Shopping	**Revision of key FC problem areas**		inversions	124
	Practice Exam 8				130
	Exam know-how				134
	Key First Certificate Collocations and patterns				136
	Phrasalperfect				147

Introduction

This book is designed to prepare students for the *Use of English* paper of the *Cambridge First Certificate in English* examination.

We felt that it would be useful to explain our approach to this preparation, as there is still some misunderstanding as to what the *Use of English* paper focuses on, tests and demands of students.

From a detailed analysis of both *Use of English* past papers and the UCLES *First Certificate in English Handbook*, it is clear that success in the *Use of English* paper **demands far more than merely a knowledge of grammar**. For the first four parts of the paper, there are three main types of item tested: **lexical** items, **lexico-grammatical** items and **grammatical** items (see below for explanations of these terms). Any effective preparation for these parts **must** focus on all three types, not just the grammatical ones. For Part 5 of the paper – word formation – there are three main types of item frequently tested: **prefixes**, **suffixes** and **irregular forms**. Students must be trained in what to expect in each part of the exam and how to 'use their English' most effectively.

EXAMS DATABASE

The structure of this book is based on a detailed understanding of the demands of the *Use of English* paper. It provides a **systematic and methodical approach** to lexical, lexico-grammatical and grammatical items for the first four parts of the exam, and focuses on prefixes, suffixes and irregular forms for Part 5.

Our first task in developing this book was to produce a **searchable database** of all items previously tested at First Certificate level since the last revision in 1996. This involved keying in items, including distractors, from all papers administered since then at UK, local and international centres. This searchable database was constantly referred to in the development of this book. It was **absolutely vital** in analysing key lexical areas, recurring lexico-grammatical patterns and grammatical structures which are frequently tested. This ensured that all items produced for this book **accurately reflect the level and content** of Paper 3. This detailed analysis also enabled us to make reasonable **predictions** of items likely to be tested in the future, giving candidates a vital **advantage** when it comes to taking the exam.

We hope the **Frequently Asked Questions** that follow will further help to explain the benefits of the structure of this book.

FREQUENTLY ASKED QUESTIONS

1 What are lexical items?

Lexical items are questions which test vocabulary. They might test the difference in meaning between discrete words, such as 'spectator' and 'witness', or they may be concerned with collocations, phrases and expressions. For example, in English we say 'green with envy' but not 'green with jealousy'. The difference between 'envy' and 'jealousy' is purely a lexical issue.

2 What are grammatical items?

Grammatical items test a knowledge of and ability to use grammar. For example, in English we say 'I moved here three years ago.' and not 'I have moved here three years ago.' The choice of the present perfect is purely a grammatical issue.

3 What are lexico-grammatical items?

Lexico-grammatical items contain both a lexical and grammatical element. For example, the difference in meaning between 'able' and 'capable' is a lexical issue. But there is also a difference in the grammatical pattern that each adjective takes. The pattern for 'able' is 'be able to do something', whereas for 'capable' it is 'be capable of doing something'.

4 What do candidates have to do in each part of the Use of English paper?

Part 1 (multiple choice cloze)
Candidates are given a text containing gaps. Each gap has four options. Candidates must choose the correct option to fill each gap.
number of questions: 15

Part 2 (open cloze)
Candidates are given a text containing gaps. Candidates must write one word to fill each gap.
number of questions: 15

Part 3 (key word transformations)
For each question, candidates are given a sentence, and a key word. They must use that key word (without changing it at all) to complete a gap in a second sentence so that the second sentence means the same as the first sentence. They are only allowed to write between two and five words (including the key word) in each gap.
number of questions: 10

Note: contractions ('won't', 'don't', etc) count as **two** words. However, because 'can't' is a contracted form of 'cannot', it counts as **one** word.

Part 4 (error correction)
Candidates are given a text. Some lines of the text are correct and some contain an extra and unnecessary word which must be identified. There are usually between three and five correct lines. Candidates tick the correct lines and write the unnecessary words in the space provided.
number of questions: 15

Part 5 (word formation)
Candidates are given a text with gaps. For each gap, the 'stem' of the missing word is given. The stem must be transformed to provide the missing word.
number of questions: 10

5 What is being tested in each part?

Part 1
- mainly **lexical** and **lexico-grammatical** items
- some **grammatical** items in the form of linkers, such as 'in case', 'as long as', 'even if' and 'while'

Note: grammatical items such as one verb in four different tenses are **not** tested in this part

Part 2
- mainly **grammatical** and **lexico-grammatical** items
- some purely **lexical** items (such as phrasal verbs and collocations)

Part 3
- mainly **grammatical** and **lexico-grammatical** items
- some purely **lexical** items (such as phrasal verbs)

Part 4
- mainly **grammatical** and **lexico-grammatical** items
- some purely **lexical** items (such as phrasal verbs)

Part 5
- **prefixes**
- **suffixes**
- **irregular forms**

6 How can teachers best prepare candidates for each part?

Part 1
- focus on topic-based **contrastive** vocabulary development, e.g. the difference between 'cash' and 'change'
- focus on fixed phrases and collocations (e.g. 'business trip' and not 'business journey') and phrasal verbs
- focus on lexico-grammatical patterns **in contrast**, e.g. 'succeed in doing' v 'manage to do'
- focus on grammatical linkers, e.g. 'even if' v 'as long as', in terms of both meaning and usage

Part 2
- focus on main grammatical items (tenses, modals, prepositions, pronouns, etc)
- focus on fixed phrases and collocations (e.g. 'go to bed', 'do one's best') and phrasal verbs
- focus on lexico-grammatical patterns, e.g. 'manage to do', 'succeed in doing'

Part 3
- focus on grammatical items **in contrast**, e.g. 'I have lived here for three years.' v 'I moved here three years ago.'
- focus on phrasal verbs
- focus on part-of-speech word formation, e.g. 'apply' to 'applicant'
- focus on lexico-grammatical patterns **in contrast**, e.g. 'manage to do' v 'succeed in doing'

Part 4
- focus on grammatical items such as auxiliary verbs, prepositions, pronouns, articles
- focus on different lexico-grammatical patterns associated with a word **in contrast**, e.g. 'study a subject' v 'study for an exam'
- focus on phrasal verbs
- focus on fixed phrases, e.g. 'green with envy' not 'green with the envy'

Note: the text in this part resembles something that a student at this level might write. UCLES suggest encouraging candidates to correct their own or their classmates' written work in preparation for this part.

Part 5
- focus on prefixes, e.g. 'honest' to 'dishonest'
- focus on suffixes, e.g. 'honest' to 'honesty'
- focus on irregular forms, e.g. 'long' to 'length'
- focus on seeing the gaps in the context of the sentence/text as a whole, e.g. 'Is a negative required?', 'Is a singular or plural noun required?'

Unit 1 Films

WARM-UP

Look at the picture.
In pairs, ask and answer the following questions:
- Have you ever watched a film this way?
- Do you think the way we watch films is changing?
- Are films getting better? In what ways?

DEVELOP YOUR USE OF ENGLISH SKILLS

A Dos and Don'ts

Which of these are good things for a candidate to do in Use of English Part 1? Which of them are not so good? Write **Do** or **Don't** before each one.

1 _____ start by reading the answers first.
2 _____ answer the questions you are sure of before attempting the ones you are not sure of.
3 _____ think about the small differences between words that are similar.
4 _____ rely on the words directly next to the gap to tell you what the answer is.
5 _____ read the whole passage to understand the gist.
6 _____ make an educated guess if you are really not sure.
7 _____ leave any items blank on your answer sheet.

B Sight and seeing

For each question, circle the correct answer.

Who ...
1 watches a film?   audience / crowd / mob
2 watches a sports event?   observers / viewers / spectators
3 looks at tourist attractions?   onlookers / inspectors / sightseers
4 watches a TV programme?   watchers / viewers / witnesses
5 sees a crime or accident happen?   sightseers / witnesses / watchers

What do you do when you ...
6 look at someone for a long time?   glimpse / stare / notice
7 look at something quickly?   view / glimpse / glance

8   watch something carefully?   see / observe / search
9   see something for a moment?   catch view of / catch sight of / catch vision of
10 see something for a moment?   glimpse / watch / inspect

C Choose the correct answer

Read the following short passages. Then, circle the answer that best fits each gap. Use the words in bold to help you.

When the (1)_____ at a **football match** all cheer at the same time or the members of the (2)_____ all laugh together at something in a **film**, they are having a very different experience from the person (3)_____ a **video** on their own. The (4)_____ of a **TV programme** are isolated from each other and can't react together to what they (5)_____.

1	A onlookers	B viewers	C witnesses	D spectators
2	A mob	B crowd	C audience	D group
3	A glimpsing	B noticing	C watching	D inspecting
4	A onlookers	B spectators	C seers	D viewers
5	A see	B search	C witness	D glimpse

I saw a great film about a woman who is a (1)_____ to a **murder**. She's driving home one day when she **catches** (2)_____ **of** two men fighting in the street. She (3)_____ a gun in the hands of one of the men **before they suddenly disappear** round a corner. She hears the shot and one of the men runs out, (4)_____ at her **for a moment**, and then runs away. She (5)_____ **which way he goes** and she follows him. It's really exciting!

1	A spectator	B watcher	C witness	D viewer
2	A view	B sight	C glance	D vision
3	A inspects	B glances	C stares	D glimpses
4	A glances	B glimpses	C observes	D watches
5	A views	B notices	C searches	D examines

D Movement and moving

Circle the correct word in each phrase.

a luxury cruise / passage on a ship
drive at high pace / speed
a round-the-world trip / outing
lose your way / route
go on a school travel / trip
take a tour / voyage round the city
a sudden burst of speed / velocity
a sudden change of way / direction
go on a business excursion / trip

cross the border / limit into a country
plan your direction / route
go straight ahead / forward
make your way / route somewhere
take / go someone to a place
lose / miss your plane
set off / set up on a journey
go at full speed / velocity

Unit 1

DEVELOP YOUR USE OF ENGLISH SKILLS

E Complete the film review

Use words from the box to complete the following passage. You may have to use the same word more than once. There is one extra word you do not need to use.

off   trip   speed   way   route   border   taken   direction   missing

Velocity is the latest film from director, James Cox. If you do make your (1) _____ to the cinema to see this, be prepared for an adventure that will leave you panting for breath! It starts when Matt, a powerful executive, leaves on a business (2) _____ for Japan, after almost (3) _____ his plane. Once in the air, a passenger with a gun forces a change of (4) _____, and when they cross the (5) _____ into Iraq and land at the airport, the real action begins. The passengers are (6) _____ to a hotel at full (7) _____, where Matt learns that he is to set (8) _____ on a journey to certain death. Great action, great acting. Don't miss it!

F Thought and opinion

Complete the following sentences using one word in each gap. You have been given the first letter of each word. Think about the words in italics to help you.

1 Her films always *give me the i*_____ that she works very quickly.

2 You'll just have to *make up your m*_____ which film you want to see.

3 Many critics *take the v*_____ that the best films are made outside Hollywood.

4 This film should appeal to those who *still h*_____ *the belief* that strong men save weak women from danger.

5 I've seen a few of his films and I've *c*_____ *to the conclusion* that he can't act.

6 If you *c*_____ *your mind* about going to the cinema, give me a call.

7 It's time we *q*_____ *the idea* that people want to see films full of crime and violence.

8 The producers finally *r*_____ *a decision* about which star they wanted to use.

9 I can't remember his name *off the top of my h*_____, but he was in that film we saw.

10 When we're choosing a video at the shop, we *should b*_____ *in mind* that George doesn't really like comedies.

G Time

Circle the correct option in the following sentences to make expressions connected to time.

1 'Don't be in such a hurry! You should keep / take your time and you'll do it right,' said the director.
2 The actors spent / passed some time preparing for their roles.
3 The film was set in the nineteenth century and, at that / such time, there was lots of poverty.
4 It's important that the actors come into the scene at the right / suitable time.
5 It'll need / take time to set up the cameras for the next shot.
6 It can be quite boring making a film and the time passes / flows slowly when you are just waiting.
7 I saw this film for the first / initial time when I was on holiday in America.
8 I don't go to the cinema very often because my homework takes up / fills out my free time.
9 You should always find / discover time to relax and watch a good film.
10 The DVD player's broken, so we can't watch anything for the time doing / being.
11 It took a considerable / lasting amount of time to get to the cinema.

H Money

Match the words to the sentences by writing the correct letter in the space provided.

1 Did you hear that his last film made an absolute _____?
2 I have to renew my _____ to *Film Monthly* next month.
3 You have to have a star in your film if you want _____ success.
4 I watch TV more now because the cinema has become quite _____.
5 Unless her next film makes a good _____, her career will be in trouble.
6 The producers decided that it wouldn't be _____ to film in the Caribbean.
7 The new cinema has started to _____ half-price for students and pensioners.
8 The shop refused to exchange the video unless I could find the _____.
9 The star was annoyed when he had to attend the film premiere at his own _____.
10 A survey shows that _____ on cinema-going has increased by ten per cent.
11 A new film studio has opened up in the old _____ area outside town.
12 He became incredibly _____ when he invested in a film that won five Oscars.
13 Most directors work hard to find producers to _____ their next film.
14 The actress demanded an increase in her _____ when they made her part longer.
15 My _____ has dropped since I changed job so I can't really afford luxuries like the cinema.

a charge
b income
c industrial
d spending
e expense
f commercial
g fee
h fortune
i fund
j economical
k dear
l profit
m subscription
n receipt
o wealthy

Unit 1

1 Choose the correct answer
Read the following passage and circle the correct word to fill each gap.

Fans of the young star, Todd Parker, are in for a treat with his next film when, for the (1)_____ time, he appears in a role that he wrote himself. He plays a (2)_____ businessman who has made his (3)_____ in the oil industry. In a sudden change of (4)_____, the businessman decides that he has had enough of the (5)_____ world and (6)_____ to the conclusion that he still has a lot to learn about life. He (7)_____ on a round-the-world (8)_____, disguised as a tramp. (9)_____ the idea that money equals happiness, the film follows the businessman as he crosses national (10)_____ and meets ordinary people. Bearing in (11)_____ that this is Parker's first attempt at writing, he should win himself new fans with this performance.

1	A first	B starting	C initial	D original
2	A valuable	B dear	C wealthy	D expensive
3	A profit	B fortune	C finances	D cash
4	A route	B way	C movement	D direction
5	A commercial	B co-operative	C commencing	D co-ordinated
6	A reaches	B comes	C ends	D arrives
7	A settles in	B turns up	C puts out	D sets off
8	A travel	B trip	C excursion	D outing
9	A Holding	B Questioning	C Refusing	D Leaving
10	A limits	B lines	C borders	D edges
11	A thought	B brain	C head	D mind

Grammar focus

Each of these sentences is about the present.
Circle the correct form of the verb in each sentence.
Then, write the correct letter in the space provided to explain why the verb is in this form.
Use each letter once.

1 Call me back later because I watch / am watching a video at the moment. _____
2 My brother always changes / is always changing the channel when I'm watching TV. _____
3 The best films teach / are teaching us something about real people and the problems they face. _____
4 We probably go / are going to the cinema about once a month, on average. _____
5 I have / am having lessons in film-making so I can use my new video camera better. _____
6 I live / am living in this small flat until I can find somewhere closer to the studio. _____
7 If you ask me, the films coming out of Hollywood get / are getting more violent. _____
8 It's a good film, but it contains / is containing some quite violent scenes. _____
9 I wish I have / had more free time to watch videos and go to the cinema! _____
10 If they spend / spent more time on the script, the films would be better. _____

A This expresses a general, scientific truth.
B This describes an action happening at the moment of speaking.
C This uses a 'state verb', not usually used in the continuous form.
D This expresses a regular habitual action.
E This expresses a temporary series of actions.
F This expresses annoyance with somebody's habit.
G This expresses a wish about the present.
H This describes a temporary situation.
I This describes an imaginary present in a conditional sentence.
J This expresses a changing or developing situation.

Exam practice — Use of English Part 1

Exam know-how

When you do Use of English Part 1:
- Remember that they often test your vocabulary in this part of the exam. Look for phrases and idioms you know and think about the small differences between the options.
- Remember that they sometimes test unusual items that you might not know very well. Often, you can say that the other answers are definitely wrong and work out the correct answer that way. If you are still not sure, make an educated guess.

For questions **1-15**, read the text below and decide which answer (**A**, **B**, **C** or **D**) best fits each space. There is an example at the beginning (**0**).

Example:

0   A carries   B holds   C takes   D makes

BREAKING INTO FILM

Hollywood **(0)** ..... out the promise of fame, fortune and glamour. Every year, thousands of young hopefuls **(1)** ..... there, hoping that a producer will spot them and think they have that special something that **(2)** ..... want to see. Unfortunately, most of them are **(3)** ..... on a journey that leads to disappointment. Take a **(4)** ..... round Los Angeles and ask any waiter or waitress and they will tell you that they are only working there for the time **(5)** ..... , until they get their break in films. A combination of failure and **(6)** ..... problems usually means that they eventually **(7)** ..... up their minds to leave and return to the small town they came from, without having made their **(8)** ..... .

Before you come to the **(9)** ..... that a life in film is for you, ask yourself carefully if you are ready for that change of **(10)** ..... . You'll have to travel and live for a long time at your own **(11)** ..... , working in jobs that provide you with a low **(12)** ..... , with only the occasional **(13)** ..... of a star to remind you where you want to be. If you do decide to make your **(14)** ..... to America with stars in your eyes, don't expect it all to be luxury **(15)** ..... and Oscar nights.

1	A send up	B turn up	C come up	D play up
2	A crowds	B mobs	C groups	D audiences
3	A making out	B setting off	C looking up	D moving out
4	A voyage	B tour	C parade	D circuit
5	A staying	B waiting	C coming	D being
6	A economic	B commercial	C industrial	D wealthy
7	A do	B make	C reach	D come
8	A profit	B cash	C fee	D fortune
9	A conclusion	B reason	C solution	D feeling
10	A way	B route	C direction	D journey
11	A money	B finance	C payment	D expense
12	A income	B earning	C charge	D wealth
13	A glance	B glimpse	C outlook	D view
14	A route	B direction	C progress	D way
15	A cruises	B travels	C expeditions	D strolls

Unit 2 Occupations

WARM-UP Pairwork

Look at the pictures. In pairs, ask and answer the following questions:
- What do you think being unemployed is like?
- What are the biggest problems?
- Are there any advantages to being unemployed?

WANTED
2 men and 2 women for work in **3-STAR HOTEL** bar and dining room. Experience preferred but not necessary! Telephone Mark on **04310 567483** for more details.

A

B

C

DEVELOP YOUR USE OF ENGLISH SKILLS

A Patterns: verbs and prepositions

In each of the following sentences, the verb is followed by a preposition. Complete each sentence by writing one word in each gap.

1. Mary refuses to allow anything to prevent her _____ becoming an actress.
2. We're hoping to start _____ the new training course next week.
3. We have a teacher at school who advises us _____ careers and job opportunities.
4. People sometimes find they are forced to choose _____ their career and their family.
5. The company accountant was accused _____ stealing money from the bank account.
6. I'm thinking of applying _____ a job at the new supermarket that's just opened.
7. He's generally regarded _____ a very good teacher by his colleagues.
8. I'm sure you'll succeed _____ whatever career you choose to follow.
9. James is always complaining _____ his job and his boss.
10. If Sam said he'd have the work done by Monday, you can rely _____ him to do it.
11. It took many years of hard work before Diane was recognised _____ a great singer.
12. Pat had to leave work early, complaining _____ a headache.
13. The boss doesn't approve _____ us making personal calls at work.
14. We hope you'll be able to take part _____ our training weekend.
15. Whether you get the job or not depends _____ your experience.
16. We would like to apologise _____ the delay in dealing with your application.
17. The manager insisted _____ interviewing each applicant personally.

B Complete the passage
Write the correct preposition in each gap to complete the following passage.

Failing a job interview
When you first apply (1) _____ a job, you might not succeed (2) _____ getting it. It's always a good idea to ask them to explain (3) _____ you what prevented you (4) _____ beating the other candidates. Don't complain (5) _____ the situation, but ask them to advise you (6) _____ what you can do better next time. Perhaps the interviewer disapproved (7) _____ or disagreed (8) _____ something you said. Perhaps they just glanced (9) _____ your application and saw something that made it easy to choose (10) _____ you and another candidate. Don't regard it (11) _____ a failure, but recognise it (12) _____ a chance to learn more. As long as you don't worry too much (13) _____ it and continue to believe (14) _____ yourself, you'll eventually find the chance you've been waiting (15) _____. Then, your family and friends will be able to congratulate you (16) _____ your success!

C Patterns: adjectives and prepositions
Match to make complete sentences. Write the correct letter on the line provided.

1 Matt decided to become a vet because he was so fond _____
2 You have no idea what you are capable _____
3 The manager is responsible _____
4 This whole area is short _____
5 Michael Jackson first became famous _____
6 Emptying the bins in summer must be quite unpleasant _____
7 I'd like to be a musician, but I'm not really keen _____
8 My ambition is to be involved _____
9 We couldn't work because the temperature was close _____
10 This part of the world is famous _____
11 Kate should make a good teacher since she's always been interested _____
12 Dad was really happy _____

a for dealing with complaints from customers.
b as a singer in the 1970s.
c for the people whose job it is.
d in the media in some way.
e for its farmers and the cheese they produce.
f to freezing outside, so we kept warm by the fire.
g at the news that he'd been promoted.
h of animals as a teenager.
i in helping young children understand things.
j of until you try.
k on the long hours of practice.
l of good job opportunities.

Use of English Skills / Unit 2

Unit 2

DEVELOP YOUR USE OF ENGLISH SKILLS

D Patterns: nouns and prepositions

Complete these phrases by circling the correct preposition.

1. at / on six o'clock
2. on / in the morning
3. on / in the evening
4. on / at midday
5. in / at night
6. on / at Tuesday
7. in / on Friday morning
8. at / in July
9. at / on Christmas/Easter
10. on / at the airport/library
11. at / in Brussels/the park
12. in / at a loud voice
13. on / at this occasion
14. a demand for / on a product
15. at / in good health
16. on / in a bus/train/plane/bike
17. on / in a car/taxi
18. in / on the first floor
19. an influence at / on somebody
20. an interest on / in something
21. on / at your way home
22. respect for / on somebody
23. 1,500m in / on height
24. the best of / in the world
25. at / in a good/bad mood
26. a talent in / for music/art
27. at / in the end of a film
28. on account for / of
29. an increase in / on prices
30. an increase on / of 10%

E Except

Sometimes the word 'except' is followed by 'for'. Sometimes it depends on the words which come next in the sentence. Circle the correct answer to complete the following sentences.

1. I get a lot of job satisfaction, except _____ those days when the boss is in a bad mood.
   a in   b on   c with

2. Nobody is allowed to leave the factory, except _____ special circumstances.
   a on   b with   c under

3. My mother works long hours and doesn't get any holidays, except _____ Christmas and Easter.
   a in   b on   c at

4. Employees are not allowed to borrow office equipment, except _____ the manageress's permission.
   a with   b on   c for

5. No exit from this part of the building, except _____ an emergency.
   a at   b in   c under

6. All applicants for the job will be called for interview, except _____ those who have been interviewed already.
   a on   b for   c that

F Complete the passage
Write the correct word in each gap to complete the following passage.

A Day (and Night!) in the Life of a DJ

Patsy Collins is (1)_____ her way home (2)_____ five in the morning after a long night, exhausted but proud (3)_____ the job she's done. Patsy works (4)_____ a DJ in the clubs (5)_____ and around Manchester and has done (6)_____ the last three years. After relaxing for an hour and then sleeping, she gets up (7)_____ around midday and a typical day begins. The first thing she has to do is listen to any new CDs that have arrived (8)_____ the post. It's very important for a DJ to keep up with the latest trends (9)_____ music. With the use of computers to make music, there has been an enormous increase (10)_____ the number of young people hoping that there is a demand (11)_____ what they produce. After choosing the tracks she is going to use, her early evening is spent getting (12)_____ the right mood. She arrives (13)_____ work (14)_____ about eleven and it's her job to get the people (15)_____ the dance floor. Six hours later, with the beat of the music still ringing (16)_____ her ears, she leaves the club and her whole day starts again.

G Discuss
Compare your answers with your partner's. Where you disagree, see if you can decide between you which answer is correct.

Use of English Skills / Unit 2

Unit 2

H Dos and Don'ts

Which of these are good things for a candidate to do in Use of English Part 2? Which of them are not so good? Write **Do** or **Don't** before each one.

1. _____ read through the whole text before you fill in the gaps.
2. _____ ask yourself what kind of word (adjective, noun, etc) is needed for each gap.
3. _____ look out for patterns you know, such as 'accuse of' or 'succeed in'.
4. _____ fill in the gaps you know to help you with the others you don't know.
5. _____ make any spelling mistakes.
6. _____ read the whole sentence to give you the context for the gap.
7. _____ read through the text again when you have filled all the gaps.
8. _____ make an educated guess if you are not sure.
9. _____ leave any gaps blank.

Grammar focus

Each of these sentences is about the past. Choose the correct form of the verb in each sentence. Then, write the correct letter in the space provided to explain why the verb is in this form. You have to use one letter three times.

1. I saw / was seeing a great programme about working on a newspaper last night. _____
2. I walked / was walking to the underground every morning when I worked in the centre of London. _____
3. I knew / was knowing nothing about being a vet until I spent the summer on a farm. _____
4. They wanted me to go for an interview on Saturday, but I had already arranged / was already arranging to play tennis. _____
5. I have been / used to go to Germany a couple of times, but I didn't like it much. _____
6. When I arrived, the other workers were discussing / would discuss the new office rules. _____
7. My mum used to travel / has travelled to work until she started to work by e-mail from home. _____
8. Dad would drive / was driving me to school every morning on his way to work. _____
9. While I was working / had worked hard, the others in the office were sitting / had sat around doing nothing. _____
10. I was tired because I had been working / was being working all day. _____

A This describes a past state.
B This describes two events that were both in progress at the same time.
C This describes a past habit.
D This describes something that happened 'before the past'.
E This describes an event in progress when another, shorter event happened.
F This describes something that happened at an indefinite time in the past.
G This describes a single event completed in the past.
H This describes something with duration that happened 'before the past'.

EXAM PRACTICE — USE OF ENGLISH PART 2

Exam know-how

When you do Use of English Part 2:
- Read the whole text before you start to complete the gaps. Then, complete the gaps that you are fairly sure about. They will help you complete the other gaps that you are not sure about. It's not always a good idea to start at the first gap and work your way to the end. Start with what you know.
- Read the whole text again when you have completed the gaps. Does it make sense? Think about what the passage as a whole is saying and ask yourself if your answers fit with the general meaning.

For questions **1-15**, read the text below and think of the word which best fits each space. Use only **one** word in each space. There is an example at the beginning (**0**).

Example: | 0 | of |

PERFUME PRODUCTION

A perfume usually consists **(0)** ......of...... an alcoholic solution containing what are known **(1)** .... essential oils. These oils are obtained **(2)** .... plants and include sandalwood and rosemary.

The essential oils are collected **(3)** .... a variety of ways, including the use of steam, the use of solvents and mechanical processes. The aroma of oranges and other citrus fruits is usually obtained by taking **(4)** .... the peel and then crushing it. Sometimes, for reasons of expense, synthetic chemicals are used **(5)** .... of natural oils. They are also used when manufacturers wish to create a fragrance that is unknown **(6)** .... nature.

Chemicals called fixatives are added **(7)** .... the essential oils to hold them together. These fixatives prevent them **(8)** .... disappearing into the atmosphere too quickly. Alcohol is then added, and the exact kind of perfume which is produced **(9)** .... on the amount of alcohol used. Cologne, for example, may contain **(10)** .... two and six percent essential oils, while aftershave can contain **(11)** .... little as half a per cent.

Each perfume is **(12)** .... up of three main sorts of smell: the top note, the middle note and the base note. Top note smells include such light aromas **(13)** .... lemon. Sage or marjoram are typical **(14)** .... the oils chosen for the middle note, while sandalwood is **(15)** .... common use as a base note.

Practice Exam 1

Part 1

For questions **1-15**, read the text below and decide which answer (**A, B, C** or **D**) best fits each space. There is an example at the beginning (**0**).

Example:

0   A although   B despite   C even   D whether

0 | **A** B C D

THE MAN WHO DREW WINNIE

Many people have seen the creations of Ernest H. Shepard, **(0)** ..... few know the name. Generations of children of **(1)** ..... ages have read *Winnie the Pooh* and *The Wind in the Willows*, and **(2)** ..... is Shepard's drawings that bring the stories to **(3)** ..... . Born in 1879, he was **(4)** ..... up in London and had a happy childhood **(5)** ..... the death of his mother when he was nine. After leaving school, he studied art at the Royal Academy and **(6)** ..... his first exhibition in 1901. After the First World War, he took **(7)** ..... a career in illustration and **(8)** ..... some of the most memorable characters in children's literature.

In his autobiography, *Drawn from Memory*, he describes **(9)** ..... it was like to grow up in Victorian Britain. He creates an excellent **(10)** ..... of life then, describing seaside visits to the **(11)** ..... and journeys by horse-drawn cab. It **(12)** ..... his own drawings of scenes from his childhood, **(13)** ..... his family life and exciting visits he and his brothers and sisters **(14)** ..... . Times have **(15)** ..... since then, but people still enjoy Shepard's beautiful illustrations.

1	A every	B all	C both	D several
2	A it	B that	C which	D what
3	A reality	B life	C creation	D force
4	A grown	B brought	C put	D done
5	A by	B though	C until	D unless
6	A put on	B made out	C came by	D turned up
7	A off	B out	C down	D up
8	A caused	B discovered	C increased	D produced
9	A how	B which	C what	D that
10	A picture	B vision	C print	D sight
11	A land	B coast	C edge	D border
12	A consists	B comprises	C composes	D includes
13	A demonstrating	B showing	C displaying	D offering
14	A went	B did	C made	D took
15	A moved	B turned	C gone	D changed

18

Part 2

For questions **16-30**, read the text below and think of the word which best fits each space. Use only one word in each space. There is an example at the beginning (**0**).

Example: | 0 | be |

WOLVES

Believed to **(0)** ......be...... an ancestor of the domestic dog, the wolf is generally regarded **(16)** .... a highly intelligent hunter. Wolves travel in packs and their territory can be anywhere **(17)** .... 40 to 400 square miles. As well as marking the borders of their territory with scent, they **(18)** .... other wolves know they are around by barking and howling.

A pack might **(19)** .... of up to 30 wolves, although where **(20)** .... food supply is limited there might only be six or seven animals in the pack. When hunting, they work together to chase an animal, block **(21)** .... escape, and finally catch it. In **(22)** .... way, they are **(23)** .... to trap large animals, such as deer or moose.

If farm animals are available, they **(24)** .... the wolves with an easy source of food. This, of course, brings them **(25)** .... contact with humans. Poisoning and shooting have contributed **(26)** .... the decline in wolf populations around the world. The red wolf is now almost extinct **(27)** .... the wild, while the grey wolf has **(28)** .... its habitat reduced to a few areas in Europe, North America and Asia. **(29)** .... many other large mammals, the wolf is increasingly **(30)** .... threat from human activity.

only 8 in 2015

Part 3

For questions **31-40**, complete the second sentence so that it has a similar meaning to the first sentence, using the word given. **Do not change the word given.** You must use between **two** and **five** words, including the word given. There is an example at the beginning (**0**).

Example:

0   You must do exactly what the manager tells you.
    carry
    You must .... instructions exactly.

The gap can be filled by the words 'carry out the manager's' so you write:

0	carry out the manager's

31 I have always admired my father for all the work he does.
    looked
    I have always .... my father for all the work he does.

32 Nobody thought the film was any good, apart from Harry.
    exception
    With .... , everyone thought the film was bad.

33 It's your responsibility to make sure all books are returned on time.
    for
    You are .... all books are returned on time.

34 'Do you realise how late it is?' Bob asked his wife.
    if
    Bob asked his wife .... it was.

35 We might be late back so take your mobile.
    case
    Take your mobile .... late back.

36 I hate the way our Maths teacher is always criticising me in class.
    down
    I hate the way our Maths teacher .... in class.

37 I'm sorry I left my book on the train.
    wish
    I .... my book on the train.

38 Why don't you use a dictionary to find unfamiliar words?
    up
    You could .... the dictionary.

39 Matt seems to be naturally good at playing the piano.
    talent
    Matt seems to .... playing the piano.

40 The Simpson twins both look exactly the same to me.
    tell
    I can't .... the Simpson twins.

Part 4

For questions **41-55**, read the text below and look carefully at each line. Some of the lines are correct, and some have a word which should not be there. If a line is correct, put a tick (✓) by the number. If a line has a word which should **not** be there, write the word on the left. There are two examples at the beginning (**0** and **00**).

Examples: | 0 | ✓ | | 00 | through |

NOT IN 2015

MY COUSIN'S WEDDING

0	✓	Last year my cousin got married to a beautiful woman called
00	through	Anne-Marie and we all went through to the wedding. It took place
41		in the summer and the church which they had chosen it to get
42		married in was really nice. We have got there about half an hour
43		early and we passed over the time chatting. The groom arrived
44		first and he looked very handsome in his new suit. I could tell
45		that he was feeling nervous because that he kept biting his nails.
46		We all went inside the church and waited for the bride to turn up.
47		When she did finally arrived, we all smiled and said how pretty
48		she looked. Music started playing out and she walked to the front
49		of the church with her father. She was wearing on such a
50		beautiful dress that she looked just like a princess. I had tears
51		in my eyes, and so did lots more of other people. The vicar read
52		the service and it was really such romantic. When the service
53		was over, the groom kissed to the bride and everyone agreed
54		with that they made a wonderful couple. They went to Bali on
55		their honeymoon and they brought me back a wonderful present.

Part 5

For questions **56-65**, read the text below. Use the word given in capitals at the end of each line to form a word that fits in the space in the same line. There is an example at the beginning (**0**).

Example: | 0 | greatly |

GETTING AHEAD IN BUSINESS

8 in 2015

Your chances of success can be **(0)** ....greatly..... increased if you follow a few simple	**GREAT**
rules in your working life. First of all, remember that your **(56)** .... wants you to	**EMPLOY**
do well – that's what you are being paid for. Many companies choose **(57)**	**AMBITION**
young people to work for them and provide a lot of **(58)** ....to their workers.	**ENCOURAGE**
Working for a large, international company may provide job **(59)** .... On the	**SECURE**
other hand, a smaller company might give you the chance to use your **(60)**	**IMAGINE**
more.	
Secondly, remember that any experience you gain will always **(61)** .... your	**STRONG**
position in the company. The company wants **(62)** .... that you want to get to the	**PROVE**
top. Take any opportunity you get to go on **(63)** .... courses related to your work.	**TRAIN**
The more **(64)** .... you are, the better chance you have of being promoted.	**QUALIFY**
Finally, don't give up, even when you are **(65)** .... Stick with it and you'll get	**SUCCESS**
there in the end.	

Unit 3

Education

WARM-UP Pairwork

Look at the picture.
In pairs, ask and answer the following questions:
- What's the best age to learn a musical instrument? Why?
- Do people find it more difficult to learn as they get older?
- Do you agree that you're never too old to learn?

DEVELOP YOUR USE OF ENGLISH SKILLS

A Dos and Don'ts

Which of these are good things for a candidate to do in Use of English Part 3? Which of them are not so good? Write **Do** or **Don't** before each one.

1 _____ read the sentence you are given carefully.
2 _____ read the words you are given on each side of the gap.
3 _____ ask yourself what they might be trying to test (indirect speech, the passive voice, etc).
4 _____ change the key word you are given.
5 _____ use more than five words to complete the sentence.
6 _____ remember that contractions ('don't', 'won't', etc) count as the same number of words as if they were written in full.
7 _____ read the whole sentence again when you have chosen your answer.
8 _____ write the whole sentence in the box on your answer sheet.
9 _____ make an educated guess if you are not sure.
10 _____ leave any gaps blank.

B The passive voice

Two schools have the same rules. One school writes its rules in the active, the other in the passive. Decide whether the sentence on the right means the same as the one on the left. If it means the same, put a tick. If it doesn't, write what the second sentence should be on the line provided.

School Rules: Active High School

1 Pupils must wear a jacket at all times.
2 Pupils should do their homework at home.
3 We expect pupils to be polite to teachers.
4 We let you keep school books for one year.
5 You must pay all fees in advance.
6 Teachers will treat all pupils equally.
7 Pupils may eat lunch in the school canteen.

School Rules: Passive Comprehensive

1 A jacket must have been worn at all times.
2 Pupils' homework should be done at home.
3 Teachers are expected to be polite to pupils.
4 You are allowed to keep school books for one year.
5 You must be paid all fees in advance.
6 All pupils will be treated equally by teachers.
7 In the school canteen, pupils may be eaten for lunch.

 Changes in tense

Rewrite each of the following sentences using the tense and the key words given.

1 I first came to this school three years ago.
   attending (present perfect continuous)

2 John last visited his old teacher two years ago.
   for (present perfect)

3 I haven't had a music lesson for six months now.
   ago (past simple)

4 Mr Platt started working as a teacher twenty years ago.
   been (present perfect continuous)

5 The last exam I took was in December.
   since (present perfect)

6 I started my homework at seven o'clock.
   since (present perfect continuous)

Use of English Skills / Unit 3

Unit 3

DEVELOP YOUR USE OF ENGLISH SKILLS

D Conditionals and unless

Match to make complete sentences by writing the correct letter a-f on the line in the left-hand column. Then, decide which sentence 1-6 means the same as each sentence A-F and write the correct number on the line provided.

1 If our school had had more money last year, _____
2 If our school has more money next year, _____
3 Unless our school had so much money, _____
4 If our school doesn't have so much money next year, _____
5 If our school had more money, _____
6 Unless our school had had so much money, _____

a we wouldn't go on so many trips.
b we would go on more trips.
c we would have gone on more trips.
d we wouldn't have gone on so many trips.
e we won't go on so many trips.
f we'll go on more trips.

A We go on lots of trips because our school is well off. _____

B We didn't go on many trips in the past because our school couldn't afford it. _____

C We might go on more trips in the future, depending on how much money the school has. _____

D We don't go on so many trips at the moment because our school has little money. _____

E We might go on fewer trips in the future if our school has less money. _____

F We went on lots of trips in the past because our school had lots of money. _____

E Reported speech

Rewrite each of the following sentences using the key word provided. Use between two and five words.

1 'Have you done your homework, Anna?' her mother asked her. **if**
   Anna's mother asked _____ her homework.

2 'You stole my school bag!' Pamela shouted at Fiona. **of**
   Pamela _____ school bag.

3 'The school closed two years ago,' Mrs Atkinson told me. **for**
   Mrs Atkinson told me that the _____ two years.

4 'I'm sorry I didn't come to your graduation,' said my cousin. **for**
   My cousin _____ to my graduation.

5 Our English teacher asked, 'Whose pen is this?' **who**
   Our English teacher asked _____ to.

6 'It wasn't me who broke the window in the classroom, Sir,' said Ali. **breaking**
   Ali _____ in the classroom.

7 'Do not forget your notebooks tomorrow,' Mrs Rogers told the class. **not**
   Mrs Rogers told _____ their notebooks the following day.

F Results

Rewrite these sentences using the phrases given. Do not change the words you are given.

1 I had to catch the bus to school because it was so far that I couldn't walk. **too far**
   _____

2 Our school was so big that you could easily get lost in it! **such a big school**
   _____

3 I got up early so that I could finish my homework before school. **in order to**
   _____

4 Andrew blamed his bad mark on being tired during the test. **was a result of**
   _____

5 If it hadn't been raining, the school trip wouldn't have been a failure. **was caused by**
   _____

G Concession

Decide whether the following statements are true or false. Write **T** for True or **F** for False. Then, rewrite the sentences using the key words given.

'Despite' can be followed by a 'that ...' clause. _F_
'In spite of' and 'despite' can be followed by the same things. ____
'Despite' is often followed by the -ing form. ____
'Although' is usually followed by the -ing form. _F_
'Despite' and 'although' are followed by the same grammatical structure. _F_
'In spite of' can be followed by 'the fact that ...' . ____

1 My school is great, although we don't have many facilities. **not**
   Despite _____, my school is great.

2 I enjoy English, despite there being so many things to learn. **although**
   I enjoy English, _____ things to learn.

3 Our teacher tries hard to explain, but I still don't understand chemistry. **of**
   I still don't understand chemistry, in _____ hard to explain.

4 In spite of his having a bad temper, Mr Turner is a popular teacher. **despite**
   Mr Turner is a popular teacher _____ has a bad temper.

H Modals

Complete the following sentences using the words in the box. Use each word only once. Do not write more than five words in each gap.

| case | long | should | might | must |

1 I expect you were very tired after your P.E. lesson.
   You _____ after your P.E. lesson.

Use of English Skills / Unit 3

Unit 3

2 You can borrow my pencil but you must give it back before the next lesson.
You can borrow my pencil as _____ back before the next lesson.

3 It's possible Wendy didn't hear what the homework was.
Wendy _____ the homework was.

4 Don't forget your trainers because we may have a P.E. lesson.
Bring your trainers in _____ a P.E. lesson.

5 Jan's teacher criticised her for not having done her homework.
'You _____, Jan,' said her teacher.

I Causative form

Rewrite the following sentences using the causative form and the key word given. Do not change the word given. Do not use more than five words.

1 They are building a new roof at our school over the summer. **built**
Our school is _____ over the summer.

2 My mum wants the hairdresser to cut my hair for the first day back at school. **get**
My mum wants me _____ for the first day back at school.

3 A teacher from another school marked our exam papers. **had**
We _____ by a teacher from another school.

4 Someone stole my money from my school bag. **stolen**
I _____ from my school bag.

5 The bell went while the photographer was taking our school photograph. **taken**
We were _____ when the bell went.

Grammar focus

Each of these sentences connects the past with the present in some way. Choose the correct form of the verb in each sentence. Then, write the correct letter in the space provided to explain why the verb is in this form. Use each letter once.

1 I have known / was knowing our English teacher since last September. _____
2 I walked / have walked to school every day for five years now. _____
3 Congratulations! You have passed / would pass First Certificate! _____
4 This is the first time I am ever being / have ever been in the staff room. _____
5 Sorry I'm late. I have been talking / am talking to the headmaster. _____
6 I am living / have been living here since 1985. _____

A This is used with a time marker, such as 'ever', 'yet' or 'already'.
B This expresses a habit that started in the past and continues to the present.
C This emphasises an unfinished continuous situation.
D This expresses a continuous action that recently finished.
E This expresses a state that started in the past and continues to the present.
F This expresses the present result of an action in the past.

EXAM PRACTICE — USE OF ENGLISH PART 3

Exam know-how

When you do Use of English Part 3:
- Think about what the question is trying to test. If you realise that it's the passive voice or the causative form, you'll be able to think about your answer more clearly.
- Remember that your answer should be between two and five words long. When you have decided on an answer, read the whole of the second sentence again to check that it means the same as the first sentence.

For questions **1-10**, complete the second sentence so that it has a similar meaning to the first sentence, using the word given. **Do not change the word given**. You must use between **two** and **five** words, including the word given.

1. I last saw Alison over a year ago.
   for
   I .... more than a year.

2. Somebody is repairing our car for us tomorrow.
   repaired
   We .... tomorrow.

3. If the CDs hadn't been so expensive, I would have bought them.
   such
   They .... I didn't buy them.

4. It's too cold to spend the day on the beach.
   enough
   It's .... to spend the day on the beach.

5. I'll lend you my car on condition that you bring it back by eight.
   long
   You can borrow my car .... you bring it back by eight.

6. The only way we can invite Emma is by calling her.
   unless
   We can't .... her.

7. Mr Edwards isn't happy, even though he has such a lot of money.
   despite
   Mr Edwards isn't happy, ... much money.

8. I started learning Russian at the end of 2001.
   since
   I .... the end of 2001.

9. Phil couldn't eat the soup because it was too hot.
   too
   The soup .... Phil to eat.

10. 'You'll fall if you're not careful,' Jamie's mother warned him.
    would
    Jamie's mother warned him that he .... not careful.

Use of English Skills / Unit 3   27

Unit 4

Sport

WARM-UP *Pairwork*

Look at the picture.
In pairs, ask and answer the following questions:
- Have you tried this sport? Would you like to?
- If you had the chance, are there any sports you'd like to take up?
- Should people of all ages take part in sports?

DEVELOP YOUR USE OF ENGLISH SKILLS

A Dos and Don'ts

Which of these are good things for a candidate to do in Use of English Part 4? Which of them are not so good? Write **Do** or **Don't** before each one.

1 _____ read the whole passage first to understand the general meaning.
2 _____ consider each sentence, not each line.
3 _____ check articles, pronouns and prepositions carefully.
4 _____ read each sentence again after you have removed any extra words.
5 _____ choose more than one extra word in each line.
6 _____ read the whole passage again to check it still makes sense.
7 _____ tick the lines you are sure contain no extra words.
8 _____ leave any boxes blank on your answer sheet.

B Tick the correct sentence

In each pair of sentences one sentence is correct and one has an extra word. Circle the extra word and tick the sentence which is correct.

1 a I am thinking of taking up tennis to get myself in better shape. _____
   b I think I need to take up a shower after playing tennis all morning. _____

2 a Once he started training, Liam turned out himself into a pretty good footballer. _____
   b Once he started training, Liam turned out to be a pretty good footballer. _____

3 a The time passed over very slowly as we waited for the match to start. _____
   b Our trainer asked me to pass the new boots over to him. _____

28

4 a Let's hope bungee jumping takes off in the next few years. _____
b Mountaineers must be careful to take off all the necessary safety measures. _____

5 a The way to win is to never give up the impression that you have lost hope. _____
b The way to win is to never give up in a situation that seems hopeless. _____

6 a My cousin got a job taking down photographs of sports events for a newspaper. _____
b A sports reporter has to be quick to take down everything the players say in interviews. _____

7 a When I got to the stadium, I joined in the queue for drinks. _____
b The other kids would never let Kevin join in their games during the break. _____

C Choose the correct answer

For each of the following sentences circle the correct word to fill the gap, or circle 'no word' if you think the sentence is already correct.

1 The world's greatest athletes should be coming _____ to the Olympics.
  a through   **b** round   **c** no word

2 My grandfather handed his football boots _____ to me when he died.
  a over   **b** down   **c** no word

3 The match is next week so we'd better get _____ to some serious practice.
  a down   **b** out   **c** no word

4 The famous footballer finally made _____ the decision to retire.
  a out   **b** up   **c** no word

5 I thought the goalkeeper did _____ a great job for the first half.
  a out   **b** off   **c** no word

6 It takes _____ a lot of courage to step into the boxing ring.
  a up   **b** on   **c** no word

7 Did you really score or are you just making it _____ to impress me?
  a out   **b** up   **c** no word

8 The coach gave me _____ permission to miss training this weekend.
  a back   **b** away   **c** no word

Unit 4

DEVELOP YOUR USE OF ENGLISH SKILLS

Circle the correct answer

Read the following passage and circle either the word given or the dash (–) if you think no word is necessary.

The Origins of Basketball

Have you any idea who came up <u>with / –</u> the idea of basketball? The origins of this sport lie <u>down / –</u> in an American student's dislike of rugby. The student was James A. Naismith and after finishing college he went <u>on / –</u> to become an instructor at a YMCA training school. He wanted to find <u>out / –</u> some way for the eighteen young men he worked with to get exercise without the violent side of most sports. In 1891, he asked the janitor to put <u>on / –</u> a couple of boxes in the gymnasium, attached to the balcony. The janitor didn't have any suitable boxes so he brought <u>off / –</u> two fruit baskets. The game quickly took <u>off / –</u> and spread to France, Canada and Australia, and was put <u>out / –</u> in the Olympics in 1904.

Circle the extra words

In each sentence, there is at least one word that is unnecessary. Circle the extra words. There may be more than one extra word in each sentence.

1 I hope we don't fall out over the discussion we had up about football.

2 It takes up a lot of time to learn how to fire out the arrows accurately in archery.

3 If we can pull off a victory in the next match, we could go out all the way to the final.

4 We are off to the park to play down a game of football, so why don't you bring about your ball?

5 Don't take off this the wrong way, but I don't think tennis is really your sport. You should try on playing basketball.

6 I look on Michael Owen as a sporting hero and try to go along to all the matches he plays out in.

Complete the sentences

Use the words from the box to complete four of the following sentences. The other sentences are correct and you should write a dash (–) in the gap to show that no word is necessary.

> off   down   through   up

1 The club decided to cut _____ on the number of tickets issued to supporters of away teams.

2 I think the council should turn _____ the land on the edge of town into a sports field.

3 The building of the Olympic village has been held _____ by delays in getting permission from the owners of the land.

4 The game against United has been put _____ until the start of next month.

5 You can take it _____ from me that this team has a great chance to win on Saturday.

6 I asked the secretary to put me _____ to the manager of the team.

G Read the passage
Read the following passage and decide whether the words in italics should be there. If the line is correct, put a tick on the left. If the word is extra, circle it and write it on the line.

Sports facilities

1 _____ Thanks for your letter. I was glad to hear that you passed *out*
2 _____ your German exam. All that work paid *off* in the end! You
3 _____ asked me about sports facilities here. I found *out* from my
4 _____ dad that they've pulled *down* the old sports centre in town.
5 _____ He used to go there to work *out* and keep in shape. We have
6 _____ some basketball courts where I sometimes play *off* with my
7 _____ friends and there are football pitches where they hold *down*
8 _____ important matches. I think they should set *up* clubs for young
9 _____ people. I bet lots of teenagers would turn *up* if they did. Well,
10 _____ I'm going to sign *off* for now. Write soon.

H Complete the sentences
Some of these sentences need a word in the gap to complete them and some don't. Either write one word to complete the sentence or put a dash (–) if you think the sentence doesn't need another word.

1 The manager said he put the team's failure _____ to a lack of preparation.

2 My dad said he'd take _____ both me and my brother skiing next month.

3 Apparently, the police are looking _____ the attacks on visiting fans.

4 I'm planning to bring _____ the question of sports facilities at the next council meeting.

5 You have to put _____ a lot of effort in if you want to become good at a sport like karate.

6 Because of school work, I had to give _____ training with the volleyball team.

7 They're planning to do _____ with free training at my school.

8 You could get a job giving _____ lessons in windsurfing.

Unit 4

1 Rearrange to make sentences

Each set of words can be rearranged to make a sentence starting with the word given. In each set, there is one word you don't need. Circle the extra word and write your sentence on the line provided.

1 take wonder I new off should I up a sport if
I _____

2 over players take to the a break decided
The _____

3 let our go early home trainer us down
Our _____

4 you lot does up a good of swimming
Swimming _____

5 wanted out to grow John be to a footballer up
John _____

Grammar focus

Each of these sentences is about the future. Circle the correct form in each sentence, according to what is being expressed.

Prediction without immediate evidence
Sport will become / is becoming more important in the future than it is now.

Prediction about the immediate future with direct evidence
That athlete will be hurting / is going to hurt himself with that javelin!

Decision taken at the moment of speaking
I think I'll take up / I'm taking up a sport to get myself in shape.

Intention
I'm going to see / I see if Ian wants to play football.

Arrangement
I'm taking part / I will take part in an important competition at the weekend.
She stays / She's going to stay in the Olympic village.

Action in progress at a future moment
This time tomorrow I play / I'll be playing tennis.

Action completed before a future moment
I will have finished / I am finishing training by seven o'clock.

Action in progress up to a future moment
In March, I will have been learning / I learn tennis for five years.

Event determined by a programme or timetable
The match starts / will have been starting at five on Wednesday.

Action referred to in a time clause after 'when', 'until', etc
I'll call you when I arrive / will arrive at the stadium.

EXAM PRACTICE — USE OF ENGLISH PART 4

not in 2015

Exam know-how

When you do Use of English Part 4:
- Remember that they often put phrasal verbs into the passage where they are incorrect. Think about all the phrasal verbs in the passage and decide whether the meaning of each one fits with the sentence it appears in.
- Some words might be unnecessary, but that doesn't make them wrong. You should only write as answers those words which make the sentence incorrect. Don't forget to tick those lines that are correct.

For questions **1-15**, read the text below and look carefully at each line. Some of the lines are correct, and some have a word which should not be there. If a line is correct, put a tick (✓) by the number. If a line has a word which should **not** be there, write the word on the left. There are two examples at the beginning (**0** and **00**).

Examples:

0	✓
00	a

SCHOOL SPORTS DAY

0	✓	I love school sports day. It's a day when we don't have to have
00	a	any lessons and we take a part in all kinds of sport. At my school,
1	✓	each class puts together different teams and we compete against
2	the	each the other. My favourite sport is the high jump and I have
3	on	represented on my class for three years now. When I took up the
4	up	high jump, I wasn't sure I could do it up at first. The other kids
5	✓	seemed very tall and I didn't think I would ever be able to jump
6	up	as high as they could. I joined up a club after school, though,
7	on	and I soon grew a bit. The training involved building on
8	✓	strength in my legs and learning how to take off properly. When
9	across	sports day finally came across, I was ready. I still wasn't as
10	✓	tall as some of the older competitors, but I made up for it by
11	over	being able to jump well. To my surprise, I took over first place and
12	up	I fell in love with the sport. Since then, I've worked up hard to
13	it	improve my technique. Sports day is next week and I hope it that
14	in	I'll be able to do in my best. Of course, now all my friends
15	✓	expect me to win so there's more pressure on me to do well.

Practice Exam 2

Part 1

For questions **1-15**, read the text below and decide which answer (**A, B, C** or **D**) best fits each space. There is an example at the beginning (**0**).

Example:

0   **A** increased   **B** grew   **C** formed   **D** developed

0	A	B	C	D

ALASKA

When Alaska became one of the United States in 1959, it **(0)** ..... the size of the USA by a fifth. **(1)** ..... this huge state, with the largest mountain in North America, has the second smallest population. This **(2)** ..... that there are still large numbers of wild animals **(3)** ..... as polar bears, moose and seals, and trapping and hunting are major **(4)** ..... . The largest group of **(5)** ..... people living in Alaska is the Inuit, who used to be **(6)** ..... as Eskimos. Most of them hunt or fish, but some of those living in cities are **(7)** ..... in government work.

Anchorage is the largest city in the state, with a **(8)** ..... of around 230,000. In 1964, large areas of the city centre were **(9)** ..... in an earthquake but the people soon rebuilt the offices and apartment buildings. Although it is only 571 kilometres **(10)** ..... of the Arctic Circle, Anchorage has a surprisingly mild **(11)** ..... . Because of its remote location, Anchorage **(12)** ..... many tourists who want to **(13)** ..... life in the wild. A **(14)** ..... number of them fly into Anchorage International Airport before hiring a pilot and **(15)** ..... into the remote areas of Alaska.

1	**A** Otherwise	**B** Despite	**C** Yet	**D** Though
2	**A** means	**B** proves	**C** demands	**D** shows
3	**A** same	**B** similar	**C** such	**D** like
4	**A** industries	**B** companies	**C** firms	**D** bodies
5	**A** starting	**B** first	**C** original	**D** native
6	**A** recognised	**B** claimed	**C** called	**D** known
7	**A** involved	**B** occupied	**C** focused	**D** included
8	**A** popularity	**B** population	**C** people	**D** residence
9	**A** collapsed	**B** dropped	**C** destroyed	**D** broken
10	**A** down	**B** south	**C** below	**D** under
11	**A** temperature	**B** warmth	**C** weather	**D** climate
12	**A** appeals	**B** attracts	**C** brings	**D** fetches
13	**A** experience	**B** contact	**C** realise	**D** look
14	**A** major	**B** considerable	**C** broad	**D** plentiful
15	**A** putting out	**B** taking up	**C** setting off	**D** letting down

Part 2

For questions **16-30**, read the text below and think of the word which best fits each space. Use only **one** word in each space. There is an example at the beginning (**0**).

Example: | 0 | about |

WHAT WE EAT WITH

Have you ever stopped to think **(0)** ....about.... the things you eat with? **(16)** .... knives have been known since ancient times, forks have been with us for a **(17)** .... shorter time. Most people in the West almost always used their fingers to eat **(18)** .... the fork became common at the end of the seventeenth century. People **(19)** .... to have knives to cut their meat and a kind of spoon to eat soup **(20)** .... , but the fork as we know it **(21)** .... days was rare. **(22)** .... , forks did exist in the kitchen. These were large and used for holding meat while it was **(23)** .... cut.

Forks for eating **(24)** .... first introduced into Europe through **(25)** .... Byzantine Empire in about 1100 and slowly spread north through Italy and France. **(26)** .... the sixteenth century, rich people in England began to carry **(27)** .... case containing a knife, fork and spoon, **(28)** .... they would use when they ate.

Through the eighteenth and nineteenth centuries, knives and forks became more **(29)** .... we know them today. They were produced in large numbers and became the traditional way **(30)** .... eating in Western countries.

Part 3

For questions **31-40**, complete the second sentence so that it has a similar meaning to the first sentence, using the word given. **Do not change the word given**. You must use between **two** and **five** words, including the word given. There is an example at the beginning (**0**).

Example:

0   You must do exactly what the manager tells you.
    carry
    You must .... instructions exactly.

The gap can be filled by the words 'carry out the manager's' so you write:

0	carry out the manager's

---

31 The match has been delayed until a week on Monday.
    put
    They .... until a week on Monday.

32 We spent the whole afternoon watching videos.
    but
    We did .... videos all afternoon.

33 Sally advised me to see a doctor.
    better
    Sally said .... see a doctor.

34 It's not worth sewing this old jumper.
    no
    There .... sewing this old jumper.

35 Prices have increased by five per cent in the last year.
    increase
    There .... five per cent in prices in the last year.

36 I last wrote to my grandma about two months ago.
    since
    It .... I last wrote to my grandma.

37 We finally managed to persuade my dad to let us go to the concert.
    in
    We finally .... my dad to let us go to the concert.

38 Although she couldn't speak French, Vanessa decided to move to Paris.
    unable
    Despite .... , Vanessa decided to move to Paris.

39 I looked quickly through the letters that had arrived that morning.
    had
    I .... through the letters that had arrived that morning.

40 Our boss said she had had enough of our arriving late.
    refused
    Our boss said she .... with our arriving late.

Part 4

For questions **41-55**, read the text below and look carefully at each line. Some of the lines are correct, and some have a word which should not be there. If a line is correct, put a tick (✓) by the number. If a line has a word which should **not** be there, write the word on the left. There are two examples at the beginning (**0** and **00**).

Examples: | 0 | ✓ | | 00 | out |

MY FIRST JOB INTERVIEW

0	✓	My first job interview was something of a disaster. I got up about
00	out	an hour before the interview, took out a quick shower and put
41		on a new suit I had bought. The weather which was awful so I
42		decided on a taxi would be a good idea. I called the taxi
43		company and they said that they would send a taxi round to my
44		house. After half an hour, I thought it was getting rather than
45		late, so I had called them back. They said that the driver
46		couldn't find my house! I gave to them the address again and
47		they promised that he would be getting there shortly. Finally, he
48		arrived and we left for the office where the interview was taking
49		place there. We had gone about a mile when there was a loud
50		bang and the car went itself out of control. The driver stopped and
51		got out. We had a flat tyre! I paid him quickly and started running
52		in the rain. I got so wet that it looked like I had been swimming!
53		I got to there twenty minutes late and my new clothes were
54		ruined. The people were sympathetic and said that they would
55		interview me anyway. I did my best one, but I didn't get the job.

Part 5

For questions **56-65**, read the text below. Use the word given in capitals at the end of each line to form a word that fits in the space in the same line. There is an example at the beginning (**0**).

Example: | 0 | certainly |

JIM HENSON

You may not have heard of Jim Henson, but you have **(0)** ...certainly... seen some of his **CERTAIN**
creations, the Muppets. Henson wanted to make education more **(56)** .... for **ENJOY**
children and to help them **(57)** .... their experience. He had used puppets a little **BROAD**
when he was at school and he first performed in an **(58)** .... show called *Sam* **EDUCATION**
and Friends. Young **(59)** .... liked the characters Henson created and he later **VIEW**
worked on *Sesame Street.* Using characters living in the same **(60)** .... , *Sesame* **NEIGHBOUR**
Street taught children about ideas such as **(61)** .... , as well as basic reading **RESPONSIBLE**
and writing skills. In the world of Jim Henson's Muppets, **(62)** .... and friendship **HONEST**
are as important as a sense of humour. The show **(63)** .... became very popular **RAPID**
with young children. The **(64)** .... of adults also enjoyed the Muppets and Jim **MAJOR**
Henson was one of the most **(65)** .... -respected puppeteers of his generation. **HIGH**

Unit 5 People

WARM-UP

Look at the picture.
In pairs, ask and answer the following questions:
- What do you think his personality is like?
- Why do you think that?
- How would you describe your own personality?

DEVELOP YOUR USE OF ENGLISH SKILLS

A Which word?

For each question, circle the correct word.

Which word ...

1 is a singular countable noun?
   a teens   b teenager   c teenagers

2 is a plural countable noun?
   a child   b children   c childish

3 is an uncountable noun?
   a advice   b advise   c advises

4 is a positive adjective?
   a attraction   b unattractive   c attractive

5 is a negative adjective?
   a impatient   b impatiently   c impatience

6 is a positive adverb?
   a abnormally   b normally   c normal

7 is a negative adverb?
   a unhappy   b unhappily   c unhappiness

8 is an infinitive?
   a approval   b disapprove   c disapproving

9 is a past participle?
   a grow   b grew   c grown

10 is a pronoun?
   a no one   b no   c not

11 is a reflexive pronoun?
   a they   b their   c themselves

B Make them negative

Complete each sentence by adding a prefix to the adjective in bold to make it negative.

1. Carol thinks that boys with long hair are really _____. I disagree! **attractive**
2. That shop assistant was so _____. I'm going to complain to the manager. **helpful**
3. Did you know that it's _____ for women to wear make-up in some countries? **legal**
4. Did you really think the exam was easy? I thought it was _____. **possible**
5. Some _____ people suffer from a lack of confidence. **employed**
6. Don't be so _____. I'm sure they'll arrive soon. **patient**
7. The report about the football match was totally _____. I was there, and there was no fighting at all. **accurate**
8. I felt very _____ when I told Darren that I didn't want to go out with him any more. **comfortable**

C Complete the table

Circle the correct negative nouns to complete the table.

Positive noun	Negative noun
1 advantage	inadvantage / disadvantage
2 approval	unapproval / disapproval
3 possibility	impossibility / inpossibility
4 happiness	dishappiness / unhappiness
5 obedience	disobedience / unobedience
6 patience	unpatience / impatience
7 ability	inability / unability
8 tidiness	distidiness / untidiness
9 belief	disbelief / unbelief
10 honesty	inhonesty / dishonesty
11 security	unsecurity / insecurity
12 certainty	uncertainty / incertainty

D Find the verbs

Look at these verbs. Five of them can be made negative by adding the prefix 'dis', e.g. 'continue' to 'discontinue'. Find the three verbs which cannot take 'dis'. Write them on the lines provided, and write their negative forms on the right-hand side.

agree   like   approve   dress   screw   prove   pack   appear

Positive form   **Negative form**

1. _____   _____
2. _____   _____
3. _____   _____

Unit 5

DEVELOP YOUR USE OF ENGLISH SKILLS

E Find the odd one out
One of the words in each group is not the negative form of a positive word. Circle it.

1 impatient   imprisoned   impossible
2 unless   unsafe   unlikely
3 disprove   distrust   disturb
4 inefficient   invaluable   informal
5 abnormal   abused   aboriginal
6 illustrated   illegal   illogical

F Dos and Don'ts
Which of these are good things for a candidate to do in Use of English Part 5? Which of them are not so good? Write **Do** or **Don't** before each one.

1 _____ read through the whole text before you choose your answers.
2 _____ ask yourself what kind of word (adjective, noun, etc) is needed for each gap.
3 _____ remember that your new word might be a negative form.
4 _____ think carefully about prefixes and suffixes.
5 _____ make any spelling mistakes.
6 _____ read through the text again when you have chosen all your words.
7 _____ make an educated guess if you are not sure.
8 _____ leave any gaps blank.

G Read and write true or false
Quickly read this paragraph about being a teenager, ignoring all the gaps. Then write **T** for True and **F** for False next to the statements below.

There's an (0) ___unwritten___ law that says teenagers find life difficult. I found being a teenager (1) _____. My parents seemed to (2) _____ of everything I did. They said I was (3)_____ and lazy. But really I was just bored and shy. I felt (4) _____ with girls, (5) _____ the ones I really liked. I remember looking in the mirror one morning and my face was totally (6) _____. The day before I'd been quite good-looking. Now I was (7) _____ and my face was covered in spots. I thought to (8) _____, 'Now I'm going to be even more (9) _____.' I just wanted to (10) _____, and I remember being so (11) _____ to be an (12) _____ adult – to leave home, get a job and earn some money. To be able to go where I wanted, when I wanted, with (13) _____ telling me what to do. For a while, I was (14) _____ unhappy. But only for a while. Then the spots went away, I fell in love, I realised my parents weren't the enemy and suddenly I didn't (15) _____ being a teenager after all. In fact, I had a great time.

1 He always enjoyed being a teenager.   _____
2 His parents sometimes criticised him.   _____
3 He says that his appearance changed.   _____
4 He wanted to stay a teenager forever.   _____
5 He wanted to feel free.   _____
6 His situation eventually improved.   _____

H Discuss *Pairwork*

In pairs, discuss your answers. Do you agree what the paragraph is about?

I What kind of word? *Pairwork*

In pairs, look at the paragraph again. What kind of word fits in each gap (adjective, noun, verb, etc)? Make notes on the lines provided. Try to note down as much information as possible.

0 *adjective – must begin with a vowel (because of 'an' before)*
1 _____
2 _____
3 _____
4 _____
5 _____
6 _____
7 _____
8 *pronoun – must be reflexive referring to 'I'*
9 _____
10 _____
11 _____
12 _____
13 _____
14 _____
15 _____

J Discuss *Pairwork*

As a class, discuss your answers. Do you all agree what kind of word is required to fill each gap?

Unit 5

K Complete the gaps

Now use each word below to form another word which fits in each gap in G.
- All of the words need a prefix.
- You may also need to change other parts of the word.
- All of the words are negatives, apart from two.
- Remember to read through the paragraph again when you have filled in all the gaps to make sure it makes logical sense.

0	WRITE	8	SELF
1	POSSIBILITY	9	POPULARITY
2	APPROVAL	10	APPEARANCE
3	ENTHUSIASM	11	PATIENCE
4	COMFORT	12	DEPENDENT
5	SPECIAL	13	BODY
6	RECOGNISABLE	14	BELIEVABLE
7	ATTRACTION	15	LIKE

Grammar focus

Complete the table of comparatives and superlatives.

REGULAR ADJECTIVES

	Adjective	Comparative	Superlative
1 syllable adjectives:	large	larger	largest
	fat		
1 or 2 syllable adjectives ending in -y:	happy		
adjectives with 2 or more syllables:	comfortable		

IRREGULAR ADJECTIVES / DETERMINERS

	Adjective / determiner	Comparative	Superlative
	good		
	bad		
	far		
		or	or
	much / many		
	little (=not much)		

IRREGULAR ADVERBS

Normal adjective	Normal adverb	Comparative adverb	Superlative adverb
good			
bad			

EXAM PRACTICE — USE OF ENGLISH PART 5

Exam know-how

When you do Use of English Part 5:
- Read the text through before and after you fill in the gaps. Otherwise, you might not notice that a word must be negative.
- For each gap, ask yourself what kind of word (noun, verb, adjective, etc) fits in the gap. If it's a noun, is it singular or plural? If it's a verb, what tense is it in? Think very carefully about prefixes. Most negative prefixes in Use of English Part 5 are 'un-'.

For questions **1-10**, read the text below. Use the word given in capitals at the end of each line to form a word that fits in the space in the same line. There is an example at the beginning (**0**).

Example: | 0 | organisation |

SUCCESSFUL WORKING RELATIONSHIPS

If you work in a large (0) ...organisation..., it is highly likely that, at certain   **ORGANISE**
times, you will have (1) .... with colleagues. Learning how to   **AGREE**
manage these successfully is an (2) .... skill.   **VALUE**

The first thing to remember is that, however (3) .... your colleague   **PROFESSION**
is in terms of his or her (4) .... , you must never lose control. Let   **BEHAVE**
them make a fool of (5) .... if they want to, but if you stay calm   **SELF**
and deal with the situation (6) .... and sensibly, things will not get   **LOGIC**
out of hand.

Secondly, don't be (7) .... to see things from their point of view.   **WILL**
Arrange a (8) .... where you can discuss your differing opinions   **MEET**
openly and honestly. Try to be as (9) .... as you can. With any   **UNDERSTAND**
luck, you'll be able to find a (10) .... to the problem, and they   **SOLVE**
may even learn something from the way you handled the situation.

Unit 6 Travel

WARM-UP

Look at the picture.
In pairs, ask and answer the following questions:
- How useful do you think travel agents are?
- How accurate do you think holiday brochures are?
- Would you like to go on a package holiday? Why/Why not?

DEVELOP YOUR USE OF ENGLISH SKILLS

A Time

Match the sentence beginnings on the left with their endings on the right. Then answer this question: What is the difference in meaning between 'spending time' and 'passing the time'?

1 We spent the whole day _____
2 It took three hours _____
3 The flight took over _____
4 While we were waiting, we passed _____
5 The time passed _____

a to reach the castle.
b sixteen hours.
c so quickly.
d lying on the beach.
e the time writing postcards.

B Complete the patterns

Look again at A and complete the grammatical patterns by circling the correct verb form.

1 time passes / takes
2 something takes / passes time
3 it takes time doing / to do something
4 spend time doing / to do something
5 pass the time doing / to do something

C Obligation and ability

Use the words from the box to complete the sentences.

| make | cause | arrange | let | allow | capable | able |

1 Grandad's over ninety now; he's not really _____ of travelling on his own any more, unfortunately.

44

2 As soon as we complained, the manager said he would _____ for us to move to another room.
3 Once I'd gone through to the departure lounge, they wouldn't _____ me go back into the main part of the terminal building.
4 They're worried the economic crisis might _____ a number of holiday companies to go bankrupt.
5 They ought to _____ travel agents give you an immediate refund if something serious goes wrong on your holiday.
6 I hope we'll be _____ to visit the Eiffel Tower while we're in France.
7 They don't _____ you to go into the departure lounge unless they've checked your ticket and passport.

D Complete the patterns
Look again at C and complete the grammatical patterns by circling the correct form.

1 make someone to do / do something
2 cause someone to do / do something
3 arrange (for someone) to do / doing something
4 let someone to do / do something
5 allow someone to do / do something
6 be capable to do / of doing something
7 be able to do / of doing something

E Obligation and ability (passive form)
Some of these sentences are grammatically correct. Some are incorrect. Tick (✓) or cross (✗).

1 After a lengthy court case, the airline was made pay compensation to the customers who had been affected. _____
2 We were made to put on lifejackets and go up on deck for a safety drill. _____
3 We were forced to take off our shoes before we could get on the plane! _____
4 We weren't let to go to the disco on our own. _____
5 We weren't allowed to go swimming there because of the sharks. _____
6 Holiday villas are let to tourists on a weekly basis. _____

F Complete the patterns
Look again at E and complete the grammatical patterns by circling the correct form.

1 be made do / to do something
2 be forced to do / do something
3 be allowed to do / do something
4 Be careful! be let = be allowed / rented

Use of English Skills / Unit 6

Unit 6

DEVELOP YOUR USE OF ENGLISH SKILLS

G Speech

Write the verbs from the box under the grammatical patterns they can take. You will write most of the verbs more than once.

> agree   announce   approve   claim   suggest   pretend
> convince   inform   mention   say   tell   persuade

announce, approve, claim, mention, say, suggest, tell ... something

_____ ... something to someone

_____ ... someone something

_____ ... something is true / has happened / will happen, etc

_____ ... someone of something

_____ ... someone about something

_____ ... to do something

_____ ... someone to do something

_____ ... of something

_____ ... doing something

_____ ... that someone (should) do something

_____ ... with someone/something

H Results and success

Match the sentence beginnings on the left with their endings on the right.

1 I managed _____
2 We finally succeeded _____
3 He achieved _____
4 Unfortunately, we failed to _____
5 This meant that _____
6 It means _____
7 The traffic jam led _____
8 This resulted _____
9 This all resulted from _____

a in getting all our money back.
b get to the Eiffel Tower.
c to catch an earlier ferry.
d to us missing the train.
e everything he wanted to on his business trip.
f in our having to get new tickets.
g we had to get up at five o'clock.
h our getting lost.
i booking well in advance.

46

I Complete the patterns
Look again at H and complete the grammatical patterns by circling the correct form.

1 manage to do / do / doing something
2 succeed to do / doing / in doing something
3 achieve to do something / doing something / something
4 fail to do / do / doing something
5 mean that - / do something
6 means do / doing something
7 lead to / in / at someone doing / do something
8 result to / in someone do / doing / to do something
9 result from someone do / doing / to do something

J Blame
Write the words from the box in the gaps to complete the sentences. More than one word can fit in some of the gaps. You can use the words more than once.

> blame   fault   criticise   accuse   charge

1 When I worked as a waiter, the hotel manager found _____ with everything I did.
2 The travel agent wasn't to _____ for the overbooking.
3 I don't think we should _____ the coach driver for driving so slowly; he was only being careful.
4 I _____ the airlines for only being interested in making a profit.
5 My dad started to _____ the taxi driver of overcharging him, but then he realised he'd made a mistake.
6 We shouldn't put the _____ on anyone; it was just an accident.
7 The police are expected to _____ the tour operator with endangering people's lives.
8 Don't _____ it on the sunshine! You should have put suncream on!

K Complete the patterns
Look again at J and complete these grammatical patterns by circling the correct word.

1 be to blame for / on / with / of something
2 blame something for / on / with / of something/someone
3 blame someone for / on / with / of something
4 put the blame for / on / with / of someone
5 criticise someone for / on / with / of doing something
6 find fault for / on / with / of someone
7 accuse someone for / on / with / of doing something
8 charge someone for / on / with / of something

Unit 6

L Choose the correct answer
Read the following paragraph and circle the correct word to fill each gap.

A traveller with Danton Airlines is (1)____ that an air stewardess knowingly left him locked in the toilet on a flight to Florida yesterday. Alan Jones, 42, (2)____ that he had a disagreement with a stewardess and then went to the bathroom. (3)____ to unlock the door from the inside, he banged and shouted for help, but was locked in for over two hours. He (4)____ to break the door down just before landing. He is (5)____ the stewardess of failing to assist a passenger, and is (6)____ the airline for employing unprofessional staff. A spokesperson for the airline (7)____ this morning that they are investigating the case. 'We take this very seriously, but there is no indication that any of our staff (8)____ to act professionally. We're not sure who, if anyone, is to (9)____ for what occurred,' he said. In a similar incident last year, a passenger was (10)____ with damaging airline property after breaking down a toilet door after being locked in.

1 A mentioning   B claiming   C informing   D telling
2 A says   B persuades   C tells   D convinces
3 A Unsuccessful B Incapable   C Unable   D Impossible
4 A succeeded   B achieved   C resulted   D managed
5 A accusing   B blaming   C charging   D criticising
6 A accusing   B arresting   C charging   D criticising
7 A announced   B approved   C told   D informed
8 A wanted   B tried   C missed   D failed
9 A blame   B criticise   C accuse   D charge
10 A blamed   B criticised   C accused   D charged

Grammar focus

Match the sentences below with the reasons A-K why each particular modal verb has been used.

1 I think we can afford to go abroad this summer.   ____
2 Angela can swim really well.   ____
3 Can I have an ice cream, please?   ____
4 Could I have an application form, please?   ____
5 He could speak French fluently when he was younger. ____
6 You shouldn't be so late all the time.   ____
7 I shall attempt to explain exactly what happened.   ____
8 I must remember to phone the travel agent.   ____
9 I knew I would look silly in this hat.   ____
10 I think it might rain later.   ____
11 Planes may be delayed at high season.   ____

A This is making an informal request.
B This is expressing a strong suggestion.
C This is expressing ability in the past.
D This is expressing a prediction in the past.
E This is expressing a future ability.
F This is expressing a possibility in a formal way.
G This is expressing a necessity.
H This is expressing a current ability.
I This is expressing an intention.
J This is making a more formal request.
K This is expressing a possibility in an informal way.

Exam Practice — Use of English Part 1

Exam know-how

When you do Use of English Part 1:
- Always think about grammar as well as vocabulary. A word may have the correct meaning but not fit the grammatical structure of the sentence.
- Think about patterns. For example, as soon as you see the word 'capable', you should think 'capable of doing something'. If you see the word 'able', you should think 'able to do something'.

For questions **1-15**, read the text below and decide which answer (**A**, **B**, **C** or **D**) best fits each space. There is an example at the beginning (**0**).

Example:

0   **A** large   **B** big   **C** heavy   **D** bulky

TOURISM

Tourism is (**0**) ..... business. Millions of people around Europe (**1**) ..... their winters planning their destination for the following summer, and their summers (**2**) ..... to foreign climes for two weeks in the sun. They are the modern-day descendants of the aristocrats and the wealthy who would (**3**) ..... months to complete the 'Grand Tour' of Europe. But unlike their forefathers, tourists these days get a bad press. They're not (**4**) ..... in the local culture, we're (**5**) ..... ; they're just after the chance to behave a bit more wildly than they do at home. What's more, they damage the local environment and don't respect the locals and their (**6**) ..... of life.

But are tourists really to (**7**) ..... ? Or is it the (**8**) ..... of the tourist industry, which has (**9**) ..... to provide reasonably-priced alternatives? And if the local resort only offers a succession of bars for the tourists to visit, can we really (**10**) ..... them for not doing more cultural activities?

One holiday company, Far and Away, (**11**) ..... that tourists are crying out for more cultural holidays and believes that it has (**12**) ..... to come up with a range of package holidays which are affordable, culturally interesting, and environmentally friendly. Their brochure, which is to be (**13**) ..... later this month, offers 200 holidays based on cultural themes, (**14**) ..... history and architecture, learning the language, meeting the locals and war and politics.

Will *Far and Away* (**15**) ..... where other companies have failed? Next summer's tourists will be the ones who decide.

1	**A** take	**B** spend	**C** pass	**D** make
2	**A** taking away	**B** moving away	**C** taking off	**D** jetting off
3	**A** spend	**B** make	**C** take	**D** pass
4	**A** devoted	**B** eager	**C** keen	**D** interested
5	**A** told	**B** informed	**C** convinced	**D** said
6	**A** way	**B** manner	**C** standard	**D** means
7	**A** criticise	**B** fault	**C** blame	**D** accuse
8	**A** criticism	**B** fault	**C** blame	**D** accusation
9	**A** avoided	**B** lost	**C** missed	**D** failed
10	**A** accuse	**B** charge	**C** criticise	**D** arrest
11	**A** claims	**B** mentions	**C** informs	**D** persuades
12	**A** succeeded	**B** managed	**C** achieved	**D** resulted
13	**A** brought up	**B** brought out	**C** brought off	**D** brought round
14	**A** comprising	**B** holding	**C** containing	**D** including
15	**A** succeed	**B** manage	**C** win	**D** accomplish

Practice Exam 3

Part 1

For questions **1-15**, read the text below and decide which answer (**A**, **B**, **C** or **D**) best fits each space. There is an example at the beginning (**0**).

Example:

0   A arrived   B came   C reached   D whether

AARDVARKS

When the Boer settlers first **(0)** ..... in South Africa from Holland, they found a strange animal. Its ears **(1)** ..... those of a donkey and its body is **(2)** ..... with stiff hair. It has a long snout, **(3)** ..... longer than that of a pig, and long eyelashes. It is also **(4)** ..... with very short, powerful legs, with **(5)** ..... it digs into the ground. The Boers named it the 'aardvark', which means 'earth pig' in the **(6)** ..... Dutch.

The favourite food of the aardvark is termites. Termites are insects that live in large colonies, **(7)** ..... ants. Using **(8)** ..... and saliva, termites construct a tall mound which is as hard as concrete. The aardvark uses its **(9)** ..... legs to break the termite mound **(10)** ..... and get at the insects inside. There are special termites, **(11)** ..... as soldiers, who try to protect the colony. Aardvarks, **(12)** ..... , have thick skin to protect themselves from bites.

Females only **(13)** ..... birth to one baby a year, so aardvarks are quite rare. When they are **(14)** ..... threat, they use their tough legs to quickly dig underground to **(15)** ..... from their attacker. Aardvarks are not often seen because they are nocturnal, sleeping in their burrows during the day and coming out to hunt at night.

1	A appear	B resemble	C seem	D look
2	A covered	B full	C decorated	D surrounded
3	A very	B more	C much	D as
4	A qualified	B enabled	C provided	D equipped
5	A which	B them	C those	D these
6	A primary	B genuine	C first	D original
7	A as	B like	C so	D also
8	A soil	B ground	C floor	D surface
9	A top	B forward	C front	D ahead
10	A out	B open	C over	D through
11	A recognised	B called	C named	D known
12	A although	B despite	C though	D still
13	A give	B make	C do	D have
14	A in	B under	C with	D on
15	A avoid	B prevent	C remove	D escape

Part 2

For questions **16-30**, read the text below and think of the word which best fits each space. Use only **one** word in each space. There is an example at the beginning (**0**).

Example: | 0 | in |

Hawaii

Hawaii, the fiftieth American state, is, **(0)** ......in...... many ways, the most unusual one. It is the only state **(16)** .... consists entirely **(17)** .... islands, **(18)** .... made up of eight main ones, together with over a hundred smaller ones. These islands are **(19)** .... tops of ancient volcanoes.

Hawaii is famous **(20)** .... over the world for its stable climate. The temperature never changes **(21)** .... much and ocean currents keep it cool, even **(22)** .... the area lies within the tropics. The western sides of the islands are dry, while further to the north, **(23)** .... the land is more mountainous, there is a high level of rainfall, in some places higher than **(24)** .... else in the world.

The stable climate and the fertile soil are the reasons **(25)** .... agriculture being an important source of income. Pineapples and sugar **(26)** .... grown all year round. Tourism is also important, although it is banned on **(27)** .... few of the islands.

Hawaii is covered with flowers the **(28)** .... year round. There are more than 1700 species of flowering plants and trees and many of them **(29)** .... been imported from around the world. You will never forget a visit **(30)** .... this island paradise in the middle of the Pacific Ocean.

Part 3

For questions **31-40**, complete the second sentence so that it has a similar meaning to the first sentence, using the word given. **Do not change the word given**. You must use between **two** and **five** words, including the word given. There is an example at the beginning (**0**).

Example:

0   You must do exactly what the manager tells you.
    carry
    You must ………………………………………… instructions exactly.

The gap can be filled by the words 'carry out the manager's' so you write:

0	carry out the manager's

31 I can't believe this is the best spot for a picnic.
    better
    There must ………………………………………… this one for a picnic.

32 The class discussed where to go on their school trip.
    discussion
    The class ………………………………………… they might go on their school trip.

33 There weren't many guests at the wedding.
    only
    There were ………………………………………… guests at the wedding.

34 I didn't know Sheila was the same age as you.
    old
    I didn't know Sheila was ………………………………………… you.

35 A mechanic is going to service our car next week.
    serviced
    We are going ………………………………………… next week by a mechanic.

36 It was unfair that Paul failed the vocabulary test.
    deserve
    Paul didn't ………………………………………… the vocabulary test.

37 I don't mind driving to work because I do it all the time.
    used
    I ………………………………………… to work, so I don't mind doing it.

38 My mum often worries about even the smallest problems.
    tendency
    My mum ………………………………………… about even the smallest problems.

39 I'm sorry I didn't visit Washington when I was in America.
    wish
    I now ………………………………………… Washington when I was in America.

40 It's possible Karen didn't hear her name being called.
    might
    Karen ………………………………………… her name being called.

Part 4

For questions **41-55**, read the text below and look carefully at each line. Some of the lines are correct, and some have a word which should not be there. If a line is correct, put a tick (✓) by the number. If a line has a word which should **not** be there, write the word on the left. There are two examples at the beginning (**0** and **00**).

Examples:

0	✓
00	to

MY FIRST PET

0	✓	I remember my first pet very well. My dad came home from work
00	to	one day with a box with holes cut in the top. I asked to him
41		what it was inside and he opened the lid. Sitting in a corner of
42		the box was a small puppy with big black eyes! He looked very
43		frightened so that I picked him up carefully and stroked him. He
44		started to lick my hand and we soon became the great friends.
45		I called him Lucky and he soon was learned to do a few things
46		when I told him to. I took him for a walk on every morning before
47		school and every evening when I got to home. It was wonderful,
48		but we soon realised that it was no much fun for him living in a
49		flat in the city. We decided to take Lucky to my grandparents'
50		house in the country so that he would have been more space.
51		We drove there in the car, with Lucky sitting on my lap. He
52		seemed like excited to be going to a new place to live and he
53		jumped out of the car as soon as we stopped. He seemed to be
54		like my grandparents and so I was happy to leave him there.
55		I see him now as often as I can see and I always take him a present, like a big juicy bone.

Part 5

For questions **56-65**, read the text below. Use the word given in capitals at the end of each line to form a word that fits in the space in the same line. There is an example at the beginning (**0**).

Example: | 0 | unaware |

E-MAIL

There can't be many people who are **(0)** ...unaware... of e-mail, even if they have never **AWARE**
actually sent one. Although there are some **(56)** .... between e-mail and letters, **SIMILAR**
there are also many differences. The first is that e-mail is delivered **(57)** .... , so **INSTANT**
it can be a very **(58)** .... means of communication when speed is important. This **EFFECT**
speed means that e-mail is more **(59)** .... for communicating over large distances. **PRACTICE**
Another difference is that e-mail tends to be **(60)** .... informal. People are much **RELATIVE**
more likely to use language which they would consider **(61)** .... for a formal **SUIT**
letter. Words spelled **(62)** .... in an e-mail are less likely to be checked than in **CORRECT**
a letter. One **(63)** .... for this is that an e-mail seems to be less permanent **EXPLAIN**
than something written on paper. We can be sure that the future **(64)** .... of **DEVELOP**
e-mail will have all kinds of **(65)** .... effects on the way we communicate. **EXPECT**

Unit 7

Food and Drink

WARM-UP — Pairwork

Look at the picture.
In pairs, ask and answer the following questions:
- How much junk food do you eat?
- Do people in your country have a healthy diet? Why/Why not?
- What health problems can be caused by eating the wrong food?

DEVELOP YOUR USE OF ENGLISH SKILLS

A Relative pronouns

Complete the following sentences using one of the words from the box in each gap. You have to use some of the words more than once. There may be more than one answer for some sentences.

> who   whom   whose   which   where   that   when   what

1 It was one of those days _____ everything I cook goes completely wrong.

2 I saw a programme about a famous chef, _____ had a restaurant in Paris.

3 Isn't that the restaurant _____ we had that wonderful meal with your parents?

4 People _____ are allergic to nuts should read labels on food carefully.

5 My new cookery book has some great recipes in it, most of _____ are vegetarian.

6 My family used to have a café, _____ became a bar after we sold it.

7 You'll find the aubergines in the bottom of the fridge, _____ we keep all the vegetables.

8 The chef's speciality is wild mushroom soup, a dish _____ he is famous for.

9 Did you get _____ I need for dinner from the supermarket?

10 He used to cook for the Queen, for _____ he created many wonderful dishes.

11 Children _____ parents can cook well are usually very healthy.

12 I love cooking for friends, _____ means I have a dinner party at least once a week.

B Modal verbs

In each of the following sentences, one of the gaps can be completed using a modal verb and the other using another kind of word. Complete the sentences. There may be more than one possibility for some gaps.

1 When you are planning a dinner party, you _____ invite people you know will get on with _____ other.

2 When I was a child, my grandmother _____ cook for the whole family while I was at school and my parents _____ working.

3 In _____ past, people didn't have fridges and they _____ to buy fresh vegetables and milk every day.

4 I realised it _____ take a lot of practice _____ I was ever going to learn how to cook properly.

5 Mum wasn't sure but she thought it _____ spoil the soup if she added more salt so she ignored _____ the recipe said.

6 If it hadn't _____ for my grandfather's influence, I _____ never have become a chef.

7 You really _____ to wash the vegetables before you chop _____.

C Prepositions

Read this short passage. Then, use the prepositions in the box to complete the passage. You have to use some of the prepositions more than once.

> over   on   down   in   from   at

Plankton

Plankton, the most basic part of the ocean food chain, is found (1)_____ huge amounts (2)_____ the oceans of the world. Slightly (3)_____ half of it consists of tiny plants called diatoms. The rest is microscopic animals and fish eggs. (4)_____ the Arctic Ocean to the Antarctic Ocean, it is relied (5)_____ as a food source by many fish. (6)_____ areas where there is no plankton, such as (7)_____ the bottom of the sea, there are fewer fish and they eat whatever floats (8)_____ to them. The small fish that live (9)_____ plankton are, (10)_____ turn, eaten by larger fish. Even larger fish feed (11)_____ them. The whole cycle of life in the sea depends (12)_____ plankton.

Use of English Skills / Unit 7

Unit 7

DEVELOP YOUR USE OF ENGLISH SKILLS

D Comparisons

These sentences all make a comparison in some way. Complete the sentences using an appropriate word in each gap.

1 Make sure you cook enough food for the party because we're expecting more _____ thirty people to turn up.

2 My daughter is actually a _____ better cook than I am.

3 It should take no _____ than half an hour for the cake to turn a wonderful golden colour.

4 Tom and Barbara's kitchen is a similar size _____ ours.

5 I might complain to the waiter because my steak doesn't look the same size _____ yours.

6 The dish will have _____ more flavour if you add a little salt.

7 The chicken hasn't been in the oven for long _____ to be ready yet.

8 This curry is far _____ spicy for me to eat.

E Pronouns and possessive pronouns

Circle the correct word to complete each of the following sentences.

1 'Why don't I drive to the restaurant in my car and Mary can go with you in _____,' Gordon suggested.
   a your   **b** yours

2 A number of dishes have _____ origins in a need to eat cheaply.
   a these   **b** their

3 Wash and chop the vegetables and, after _____, heat the oven to 300 degrees centigrade.
   a that   **b** these

4 Your kitchen is quite modern, whereas _____ is very traditional.
   a my   **b** mine

5 This dish will be popular with _____ who like strong flavours.
   a they   **b** those

F Auxiliary verbs

Complete each of the following sentences using an appropriate form of 'have', 'do' or 'be'.

1 I have always _____ fascinated by the eating habits of other cultures.

2 My dad spends little time in the kitchen, but he _____ cook when we have guests for dinner.

3 By the end of the twentieth century, foreign food _____ become familiar in British supermarkets.

4 You've made so much food that you must _____ been cooking all morning.

5 The taste of frogs' legs could _____ described as rather like chicken.

6 There is still a lot to _____ learnt about the relationship between our diet and our health.

7 This cocktail _____ created at the bar of the Hilton Hotel in the thirties.

8 After _____ peeled and chopped the vegetables, place them in boiling water for fifteen minutes.

9 I like Italian food, although some of it _____ seem to me to be a bit basic.

10 Apart from _____ very tasty, a lot of fast food doesn't really have any other positive points.

G Articles

Circle the word which best completes each sentence.

1 Brazil is our / the / a world's largest exporter of coffee.

2 It is a / the / one fact that the human body needs a balanced diet.

3 Our trip to China was the / a / an unique opportunity to try authentic Chinese food.

4 The diet of European people improved with one / the / an introduction of new vegetables from America, such as potatoes.

5 It's not clear why we suffer from heart attacks in the West, although a / one / the reason must be our diet.

6 Indigestion is a / the / this common result of eating too much spicy food.

Unit 7

 Find the missing words
Complete the following passage using an appropriate word in each gap. You are told before each gap what kind of word is missing.

How snakes eat

Different snakes catch (*possessive pronoun*) _____ food (*preposition*) _____ different ways. The constrictors, (*relative pronoun*) _____ are large, powerful snakes like the python, wrap themselves around animals and squeeze (*pronoun*) _____. Others, such as (*article*) _____ viper, use special teeth called fangs to inject poison (*preposition*) _____ their victims.
(*auxiliary verb*) _____ caught an animal, the snake opens (*possessive pronoun*) _____ jaws extremely wide and swallows it whole, usually head first. It (*modal*) _____ take more than an hour to swallow a large meal. Because food sources are unpredictable, many snakes (*auxiliary verb*) _____ evolved the ability to survive (*preposition*) _____ long periods without food. Fat can (*auxiliary verb*) _____ stored in the body to provide energy when other sources of food are unavailable.

Grammar *focus*

In each of the following sentences, circle the correct modal verb. Then circle the best description of the meaning of the sentence.

1. I think I should / would have cooked more food. There's nothing left, now!
   a. I didn't do something and I think that was a mistake.
   b. It's possible I did something, but I'm not sure.

2. You must / could have told me you were going to be late for dinner.
   a. Judging by the evidence, I'm sure you didn't do something.
   b. You didn't do something and I think that was a mistake.

3. Looks like Dad may / can't have forgotten to add salt to the soup again.
   a. Dad definitely forgot to add salt.
   b. It's possible that Dad forgot to add salt.

4. You really needn't / mustn't have cooked so much food – we're on a diet.
   a. It's good that you didn't cook too much food.
   b. It wasn't necessary to cook a lot of food, even though you did.

5. You needn't / can't have added any garlic or we'd be able to taste it.
   a. Judging by the evidence, I'm sure you didn't do something.
   b. It's possible you did something but I'm not sure.

6. It would / must have been a great meal, if the restaurant hadn't been so cold.
   a. The restaurant wasn't cold and the meal was great.
   b. The restaurant was cold and that spoiled the meal.

7. There's no milk left. Somebody should / must have drunk it.
   a. Judging by the evidence, I'm sure somebody drank the milk.
   b. It's possible somebody drank the milk, but I'm not sure.

8. You really ought to / had to have asked Sarah if she liked pork before you started cooking.
   a. You didn't do something and I think that was a mistake.
   b. Judging by the evidence, I'm sure you asked Sarah a question.

9. There might / needn't have been about thirty people at the party but I didn't count them.
   a. It's possible there were thirty people but I'm not sure.
   b. It was a mistake to invite so many people to the party.

EXAM PRACTICE — USE OF ENGLISH PART 2

Exam know-how

When you do Use of English Part 2:
- Remember that the missing words are often 'grammatical' words, like articles, prepositions, auxiliary verbs and pronouns. Try to work out what kind of word is needed in each gap.

- You might be able to think of two different words for a gap, both of which seem correct. Read the sentence twice, once with each word in the gap, and decide which sounds better. Do not write both words on your answer sheet. Some gaps have more than one correct answer but you should only write one word on your answer sheet for each gap.

For questions **1-15**, read the text below and think of the word which best fits each space. Use only **one** word in each space. There is an example at the beginning (**0**).

Example: | 0 | still |

TEA

Britain is **(0)** ......*still*...... the biggest importer of tea, although **(1)** .... more coffee is drunk there than used to **(2)** .... Since 1660, **(3)** .... it was first introduced into England, tea **(4)** .... been widely drunk and it became more popular **(5)** .... ever as the British Empire grew.

China and India produce **(6)** .... majority of the world's tea, although other countries, **(7)** .... as Sri Lanka and Japan, are also important. The young leaves are picked and taken **(8)** .... a factory, where they are spread **(9)** .... and allowed to dry. They are then sent to a rolling machine, **(10)** .... breaks the leaf cells and releases oils which give the tea its flavour. Then, the leaves are left to absorb oxygen and they turn **(11)** .... bright copper colour before being heated in an oven and turning black.

A lot of tea **(12)** .... days is prepared using tea bags. These were invented **(13)** .... accident at the start of the twentieth century. Thomas Sullivan of New York decided to send samples to his customers in small cloth bags and the customers thought that they **(14)** .... to use the bags to make tea. It worked **(15)** .... well that tea bags have been popular ever since.

Unit 8

WARM-UP

Look at the picture.
In pairs, ask and answer the following questions:
- How do you think the people in the photograph feel?
- Do you think that famous people have a right to a private life?
- Do you like reading about the private lives of celebrities?

The Media

DEVELOP YOUR USE OF ENGLISH SKILLS

A Complete the phrasal verbs

Write the verbs from the box in the gaps to complete these sentences. You will use some of the verbs more than once.

> took   cut   put   turned   looked   pulled   ran

1 The journalists _____ **up with** the managing editor's reorganisation of the department for a long time before they started complaining.

2 The paper _____ **down on** the number of reporters stationed in foreign countries in an attempt to save money.

3 Someone in the street _____ me **for** that TV presenter Angela Dimble and asked for my autograph. I guess we do look similar!

4 When they offered me *The Breakfast Show*, I initially _____ it **down**. I didn't fancy getting up so early every morning!

5 The receptionist _____ me **through** to the wrong department by mistake, so I had to call back.

6 The MTV Music Awards _____ **place** in Los Angeles this year.

7 We always _____ **up to** Peter – he was one of the best war correspondents in the history of television.

8 They _____ **down** that old TV studio last week. Apparently, they're going to build a supermarket in its place.

9 Some friends kindly _____ me **up** for a few days while I was there. It was much nicer than staying in a hotel.

10 The newsagent _____ **out of** copies of *TeenPop* on the first day of its publication, so he had to order more.

B Match

Match each of these verbs and phrases with a phrasal verb in bold from A that means approximately the same thing. Write the numbers of the sentences 1-10 on the lines provided.

A respected   _____
B didn't have any left   _____
C demolished   _____
D connected   _____
E tolerated   _____
F didn't accept   _____
G reduced   _____
H was held   _____
I thought someone was _____
J provided accommodation _____

C Complete the sentences

Complete the following sentences using the word given. You must use between two and five words, including the word given.

1 People often think Karen is Madonna. **taken**
   Karen _____ Madonna.

2 Newspapers should reduce the amount of un-recycled paper they use. **cut**
   Newspapers should _____ the amount of un-recycled paper they use.

3 I've had enough of your rudeness – you're fired! **put**
   I refuse to _____ any more – you're fired!

4 Could you connect me to the newsroom, please? **put**
   Could _____ to the newsroom, please?

5 They held the ceremony at a concert hall in London. **took**
   The ceremony _____ at a concert hall in London.

6 I have a lot of respect for journalists who put themselves in danger. **look**
   I really _____ journalists who put themselves in danger.

7 Can I stay with you for a couple of days next week while I'm in town? **put**
   Could _____ for a couple of days next week while I'm in town?

8 There aren't any more *Guardian* newspapers left, I'm afraid. **run**
   I'm afraid we _____ *Guardian* newspapers.

Unit 8

DEVELOP YOUR USE OF ENGLISH SKILLS

D Nouns from verbs
Write the nouns from the verbs to complete the table.

Verbs	Nouns	Verbs	Nouns
1 apply		8 permit	
2 visit		9 discuss	
3 sing		10 solve	
4 swim		11 describe	
5 appear		12 tend	
6 agree		13 intend	
7 behave			

E Nouns from adjectives
Write the nouns from the adjectives to complete the table.

Adjectives	Nouns
1 accurate	
2 difficult	
3 responsible	
4 kind	
5 rude	

F Circle the correct words
Circle the correct words to complete these phrases.

1 have / get difficulty in / at doing something
2 have / do a discussion of / about something
3 do / find a solution of / to something
4 make / give a description of / about something
5 be / have responsibility for / of something
6 get / be in agreement with / to something
7 have / do a tendency to do / for doing something

G Complete the sentences
Complete the following sentences using the word given. You must use between two and five words, including the word given.

1 Only a few people applied for the job of editorial assistant. **many**
   There weren't _____ the job of editorial assistant.

2 The band became very successful after they appeared on TV. **following**
   The band became very successful _____ on TV.

3 She found it difficult to arrange an interview with the Prime Minister. **difficulty**
   She _____ an interview with the Prime Minister.

62

4 She often asks difficult questions in interviews. **tendency**
She _____ difficult questions in interviews.

5 We've got to solve this problem somehow. **find**
We must _____ to this problem somehow.

6 The panel discussed the latest political issues. **discussion**
The panel _____ the latest political issues.

H Complete the words
Complete the words so that the second sentence means the same as the first.

1 a I'd like to know whether radio is increasing in popularity again.
  b I w_____ whether radio is increasing in popularity again.

2 a I'm not at all interested in working in the media.
  b Working in the media doesn't i_____ me at all.

3 a I have examined your report very carefully.
  b I've taken a careful l_____ at your report.

4 a Simon didn't need to rewrite much of the article.
  b It wasn't n_____ for Simon to rewrite much of the article.

5 a I wrote down some questions I wanted to ask.
  b I made a n_____ of some questions I wanted to ask.

6 a We have to concentrate on increasing our readership.
  b We have to pay a_____ to increasing our readership.

7 a The editorial said the government had caused the crisis.
  b The editorial b_____ the government for causing the crisis.

8 a My boss said I could take the day off.
  b My boss gave me p_____ to take the day off.

I Complete the sentences
Write the words from the box in the gaps to complete the sentences.

> go   tell   work   remember   receive   hear   lend   arrive

1 If you borrow something from someone, they _____ it to you.

2 If you are employed by someone, you _____ for them.

3 If someone contacts you, you _____ from them.

4 If you are punctual, you don't usually _____ late.

5 If someone sends you a letter, you _____ it.

6 If someone makes you stay in, they don't let you _____ out.

7 If you forgot to do something, you didn't _____ to do it.

8 If two things look exactly the same, you can't _____ the difference between them.

Use of English Skills / Unit 8

Unit 8

J **Complete the sentences**
Complete the following sentences using the word given. You must use between two and five words, including the word given.

1. Dave's usually so punctual. **like**
   It's _____ so late.

2. These two photos look exactly the same to me. **difference**
   I can't _____ these two photos.

3. Jan was going to cancel the papers when she went on holiday, but she forgot. **remember**
   Jan _____ the papers when she went on holiday.

4. I haven't received the catalogue yet. **still**
   The company _____ the catalogue.

5. My parents made me stay at home last Saturday night. **let**
   My parents _____ out last Saturday night.

Grammar focus

Circle the correct word or phrase to complete the sentences on the right.

	direct speech	reported speech
1	'I am a peaceful person,' said Ghandi.	Ghandi said he <u>was</u> / <u>is</u> a peaceful person.
2	'Are we winning the battle?' asked Julius Caesar.	Julius Caesar asked if his side <u>is</u> / <u>was</u> winning the battle.
3	'You've annoyed me, Peter,' said Helen.	Helen told Peter that he <u>has</u> / <u>had</u> annoyed her.
4	'I didn't think it would end like this,' said Napoleon.	Napoleon said that he <u>hasn't</u> / <u>hadn't</u> thought it would end like <u>this</u> / <u>that</u>.
5	'I was joking about the Earth being flat,' said Galileo.	Galileo said he <u>was being</u> / <u>had been</u> joking about the Earth being flat.
6	'I think my music will be remembered for a long time,' said Elvis.	Elvis said he <u>thought</u> / <u>thinks</u> his music <u>will</u> / <u>would</u> be remembered for a long time.
7	'I can see into the future,' said Nostradamus.	Nostradamus said that he <u>can</u> / <u>could</u> see into the future.
8	'I must try,' said David.	David said that he <u>must</u> / <u>had</u> to try.
9	'I may write a play one day,' said William Shakespeare to his mother.	William Shakespeare told his mother that he <u>may</u> / <u>might</u> write a play one day.
10	'Don't worry!' said the Captain to his guests. 'Titanic is unsinkable.'	The Captain told his guests <u>not to</u> / <u>to not</u> worry as Titanic <u>was</u> / <u>is</u> unsinkable.
11	'What did it feel like to be the first man on the Moon?' the reporter asked Neil Armstrong.	Neil Armstrong was asked what <u>had it felt</u> / <u>it had felt</u> like to be the first man on the Moon.
12	'Why can't we live in peace?' wondered John Lennon.	John Lennon wondered why <u>we couldn't</u> / <u>couldn't we</u> live in peace.
13	'Do you want to be in my next movie?' asked Steven Spielberg.	Steven Spielberg asked if I <u>wanted</u> / <u>did want</u> to be in his next movie.
14	'I'll go home tomorrow,' said Jenny.	Jenny said that she <u>will</u> / <u>would go</u> home <u>tomorrow</u> / <u>the next day</u>.
15	'I wish someone would run me a nice bath of milk,' thought Cleopatra.	Cleopatra wished that someone would <u>have run</u> / <u>run</u> her a bath of milk.

Exam Practice — Use of English Part 3

Exam know-how

When you do Use of English Part 3:
- Remember that contractions ('won't', 'shouldn't', 'didn't', etc) count as two words, not one. However, there is one exception to this rule. Because 'can't' means 'cannot', it only counts as one word.
- Make sure you include all the information from the first sentence in your new sentence. For example, if something was 'described in detail' and you have to use the word 'description', you should write 'a detailed description' and not just 'a description'.

For questions **1-10**, complete the second sentence so that it has a similar meaning to the first sentence, using the word given. **Do not change the word given**. You must use between **two** and **five** words, including the word given.

1. I'll always remember how kind Harry was to me when I first started working there.
   never
   I'll .... to me when I first started working there.

2. Kylie can't swim as well as Jason.
   good
   Kylie is not .... Jason.

3. The twins behaved so badly last night.
   bad
   The twins' .... last night.

4. No one has applied for the job yet.
   any
   I .... for the job yet.

5. Sally had great difficulty in accepting the situation.
   really
   Sally found .... the situation.

6. The witness gave a detailed description of the bank robber's appearance.
   in
   The witness .... the bank robber's appearance.

7. Bella has examined the information carefully.
   taken
   Bella .... at the information.

8. It's Mr Peters' duty to deal with overseas students.
   responsibility
   Mr Peters .... with overseas students.

9. I won't tolerate your being rude any longer.
   put
   I'm not going to .... any longer.

10. Adrian hasn't accepted the offer, unfortunately.
    down
    Adrian ...., unfortunately.

Practice Exam 4

Part 1

For questions **1-15**, read the text below and decide which answer (**A, B, C** or **D**) best fits each space. There is an example at the beginning (**0**).

Example:

0   **A** West   **B** Westerly   **C** Western   **D** Westward

| 0 | A | B | C | D |

CREDIT CARDS

In most (0) ….. countries, few people use cash any more to pay for large purchases. (1) ….. , they either write cheques or pay by credit card. Whereas cheques are decreasing in (2) ….. each year, the credit card has become increasingly indispensable. Many people now have several credit cards at any one time.

Paying by credit card offers (3) ….. several major advantages. Firstly, you don't have to carry around large amounts of (4) ….. (which could be stolen and is (5) ….. to have in your pocket or wallet) or a large cheque book. Secondly, unlike cheques, you usually have several weeks in which to (6) ….. pay. This is because of the way the system (7) ….. . With a credit card, you receive a (8) ….. from the credit card company or bank at the end of each month. If you (9) ….. your purchase at the beginning of the month, you will have had several weeks of interest-free credit. You can then decide to pay the amount in (10) ….. , and thus not be charged any interest at all, or to only pay a (11) ….. amount, delaying the remainder of the payment, at a high (12) ….. of interest, to subsequent months.

This, of course, can lead to one of the main disadvantages of credit cards. They (13) ….. people the impression that they can (14) ….. to spend more than they actually can, (15) ….. in their ending up with huge amounts of debt.

1	**A** Likewise	**B** Rather	**C** However	**D** Moreover
2	**A** fame	**B** reputation	**C** regard	**D** popularity
3	**A** shoplifters	**B** regulars	**C** consumers	**D** clients
4	**A** cash	**B** currency	**C** exchange	**D** coinage
5	**A** annoying	**B** bothering	**C** disturbing	**D** disrupting
6	**A** actually	**B** really	**C** truly	**D** rightly
7	**A** happens	**B** acts	**C** works	**D** manages
8	**A** fee	**B** bill	**C** charge	**D** receipt
9	**A** took	**B** did	**C** created	**D** made
10	**A** total	**B** complete	**C** whole	**D** full
11	**A** clear	**B** sure	**C** certain	**D** firm
12	**A** grade	**B** worth	**C** value	**D** rate
13	**A** give	**B** make	**C** take	**D** have
14	**A** provide	**B** succeed	**C** afford	**D** achieve
15	**A** resulting	**B** leading	**C** affecting	**D** forcing

Part 2

For questions **16-30**, read the text below and think of the word which best fits each space. Use only **one** word in each space. There is an example at the beginning (**0**).

Example: | 0 | among |

OLIVES

The olive tree is (**0**) ...*among*... the longest-living trees known in Europe. It can grow (**16**) .... an age of 1500 years and has (**17**) .... valued since ancient times for its fruit. It is cultivated in the Mediterranean, as well (**18**) .... in other places like South America and Australia.

Fresh olives are inedible and have (**19**) .... very bitter taste. In order to get (**20**) .... of this bitterness, three main methods are used: Greek, Spanish and American. In the Greek method, the mature fruit are put in brine for (**21**) .... to six months, (**22**) .... being left in the open air to give (**23**) .... back their dark colour. They are then packed in fresh brine to be sold. In the Spanish and American methods, the fruit is harvested much earlier (**24**) .... in the Greek method, producing a sweeter fruit which is often green (**25**) .... colour.

The olives may also (**26**) .... pressed to produce olive oil, (**27**) .... is used in cooking. Italian, Spanish and Greek cuisines all (**28**) .... use of this oil, giving Mediterranean dishes a unique flavour. (**29**) .... is supposed to be healthier than other cooking oils and is sometimes given as one reason (**30**) .... people in Mediterranean countries seem not to suffer from heart attacks in high numbers.

Part 3

For questions **31-40**, complete the second sentence so that it has a similar meaning to the first sentence, using the word given. **Do not change the word given.** You must use between **two** and **five** words, including the word given. Here is an example (**0**).

Example:

0 You must do exactly what the manager tells you.
carry
You must .... instructions exactly.

The gap can be filled by the words 'carry out the manager's' so you write:

0	carry out the manager's

---

31 Fishing really doesn't interest me at all.
not
I'm .... fishing.

32 I don't like you spending so much time on your computer.
wish
I .... so much time on your computer.

33 Kay's favourite subject at school was physics.
most
The subject .... at school was physics.

34 'Don't leave your dirty clothes on the floor, Tom,' his mum said.
not
Tom's mum .... his dirty clothes on the floor.

35 The students all wrote down the words from the blackboard.
note
The students all .... the words from the blackboard.

36 I suggest that you allow Tony to come to the party.
let
Why .... come to the party?

37 Promise to look after it and you can borrow my tennis racquet.
long
You can borrow my tennis racquet, ... to look after it.

38 The wedding was held despite the rain.
place
The wedding .... it was raining.

39 The film camera was invented by an American.
who
It .... the film camera.

40 The books you found on the bus aren't mine.
to
The books you found on the bus .... me.

Part 4

For questions **41-55**, read the text below and look carefully at each line. Some of the lines are correct, and some have a word which should not be there. If a line is correct, put a tick (✓) by the number. If a line has a word which should **not** be there, write the word on the left. There are two examples at the beginning (**0** and **00**).

Examples:

0	✓
00	over

MY HOBBY

0	✓	I've got a very interesting and enjoyable hobby. I make short
00	over	films with my video camera. I saved up for the camera for over
41	did	months, and did finally bought it late last year. Since then, I have
42	✓	made three films, each one about forty-five minutes long. It's
43	✓	great fun! I start by asking my friends and relations if they want
44	part	to be part in the film. They usually do, unless they're not
45	what	available on the days I'm planning what to do the filming. When I
46	that	know that who the actors will be, I think of the plot and write the
47	off	script. I usually set off the story in the present day so I don't have
48	will	to worry too much about costumes. Once I will have finished the
49	✓	script, I make photocopies for all the actors and give them to
50	of	them, asking of them to learn their lines before we start filming. It
51	✓	doesn't really matter, though, if they haven't learnt all their lines.
52	a	Each scene is quite a small and they can look at the words just
53	to	before we start to filming. We film at the weekend in my local
54	do	neighbourhood, so no one has to do travel far. After editing, the
55	✓	film is ready. I will invite all the actors and we watch the film at my house.

Part 5

For questions **56-65**, read the text below. Use the word given in capitals at the end of each line to form a word that fits in the space in the same line. There is an example at the beginning (**0**).

Example: | 0 | amusement |

ZOOS

The days when people would go to a zoo simply for **(0)** amusement are long gone. Today, **AMUSE**
when we place greater **(56)** importance on the survival of animals in the wild, zoos have **IMPORT**
a duty to inform the public and improve our **(57)** knowledge of the environment and the **KNOW**
problems faced **(58)** worldwide by large numbers of animals. Today's zoos also play a role **WORLD**
in the **(59)** protection of threatened species, breeding animals for release in the wild. Many **PROTECT**
zoos also fund **(60)** scientific research into animals and their behaviour. The way animals **SCIENCE**
are treated in zoos has changed, too. Many intelligent animals suffer from **(61)** boredom **BORE**
in captivity and their keepers now try to improve the **(62)** psychological state of the animals in **PSYCHOLOGY**
their care. They do this by, for example, providing the animals with a **(63)** variety of **VARY**
different food or by changing the animals' **(64)** daily routine. Although some critics of **DAY**
zoos remain **(65)** unconvinced, there can be no doubt that animals in zoos today enjoy a **CONVINCE**
more comfortable existence than in the past.

Unit 9
The Weather

WARM-UP

Look at the picture.
In pairs, ask and answer the following questions:
- What problems can be caused by the weather?
- What measures do people take to protect themselves from the weather?
- How does the weather affect our way of life?

DEVELOP YOUR USE OF ENGLISH SKILLS

A Tick the correct sentence

Each of these sentences refers to time. In each pair of sentences one sentence is correct and one has an extra word. Circle the extra word and tick the sentence which is correct.

1. a It was raining all the night and once I was awake I couldn't get back to sleep. _____
   b There was a terrible storm during the night and it really frightened me. _____

2. a It'll take us about a quarter of an hour to get there, unless the weather is bad. _____
   b We'll be leaving in half of an hour, if this shower passes. _____

3. a I couldn't go to school all the last week because of the snow. _____
   b The school had been closed all the week before because of the deep snow. _____

4. a We arrived at the hotel just in the time to avoid the thunderstorms. _____
   b An inch of snow fell just in the time it took us to get home. _____

5. a I have Monday free day so, if the weather's okay, we could go for a picnic. _____
   b Let's try and arrange a time to go for a picnic, if you have a free day next week. _____

6. a My dad went fishing at the weekend and he said it rained the whole time. _____
   b I'll meet you at the midday and we'll set off for the lake, if it isn't too cold. _____

7 a Repairing the fence will take about an hour's more work, depending on the weather.   ____
   b The rain is getting less heavy, so I think we'll be there in about an hour's more time.   ____

B Find the extra word

Each of these sentences refers to quantity and has one extra word. Find it and circle it.

1. It was a bit of strange for it to be so cold that the sea froze.
2. A quite lot of rain falls on the mountains in this area in the summer.
3. I would say that it has been raining constantly for ten days, at very least.
4. There should be plenty more to do on holiday, as long as the weather stays fine.
5. It seems that many lots of very young kids are afraid of thunder and lightning.
6. When it snowed, my friends called to see if I wanted to go skiing with all them.
7. I've had enough of all this rain and I can't wait to go on holiday, if I've got enough of money.
8. The recent bad weather has caused a great deal extra of trouble in the north of the country.
9. If you don't like the colour of this one, Madam, we've got plenty more than umbrellas in the stock room.
10. We got home much over an hour later than we expected on account of the dreadful weather.

C Circle the correct answer

Read the following passage and circle either the word given or the dash (–) if you think no word is necessary.

Weather data

Data on the weather is collected from all / – over the world. Meteorologists work all / – around the clock, recording temperatures and wind speeds. Weather satellites take pictures of all / – the whole Earth, even if / – the North and South Poles. These pictures provide information on weather conditions, even though / – they are taken from far / – away. A lot of this information is available all / – over the internet so that even though / – ordinary people can see what the weather is like on the far / – opposite side of the world. Forecasters can analyse weather patterns and even they / – predict the weather up to ten days far / – in advance with some certainty.

Unit 9

DEVELOP YOUR USE OF ENGLISH SKILLS

D Complete the sentences

Use the word 'of' to complete three of the following sentences. The other sentences are correct and you should write a dash (–) in the gap to show that no word is necessary.

1 It was too cold in Russia for my dad so instead _____ we are going to Florida on holiday.

2 We had to turn back because _____ the bad weather which had developed suddenly.

3 We decided to delay our trip because _____ the heavy rain made driving difficult.

4 Take your raincoat in case _____ heavy showers.

5 Let's go outside and play in the rain instead _____ just sitting in here with nothing to do.

6 Don't forget your umbrella in case _____ it starts raining.

E Read the passage

Read the following passage and decide whether the words in italics should be there. If the word is correct, put a tick on the left. If the word is extra, circle it and write it on the line.

Wanting to be a meteorologist

1 _____ I applied *myself* for a job as a meteorologist three years ago
2 _____ and they rejected me. The manager insisted *on* that I got more
3 _____ experience and he advised me *on* what things I should do.
4 _____ I was keen *on* to learn from his experience and to find out
5 _____ just what being a meteorologist involved *in*. He suggested
6 _____ that I visit some weather stations and discuss *about* the work
7 _____ they do with the people there. Because *of* I'm still young, he
8 _____ thought *of* it would be a good idea to go to university and
9 _____ study meteorology. He explained *that* you have to understand
10 _____ a lot *of* about climate before you can forecast the weather.

F Choose the correct answer

For each of the following sentences circle the correct word to fill the gap, or circle 'no word' if you think the sentence is already correct.

1 It seems _____ to be starting to snow on the mountains.
   a that   b me   c no word

2 The weather was so bad that we were in need _____ another holiday.
   a for   b of   c no word

3 The damp weather has damaged the house, as _____ you can see from this wall.
   a though   b if   c no word

4 As soon as we arrive _____ there, I want to change out of these wet clothes.
   a to   b at   c no word

5 The weather seems to really affect _____ my mood and I'm always depressed in winter.
   a to   b on   c no word

6 Our grandmother insisted _____ us wearing our jackets to go out into the cold.
   a that   b on   c no word

7 The pilot told _____ passengers that he was expecting rough weather ahead.
   a to   b them   c no word

8 I hope _____ to go on holiday to India once the rainy season ends there.
   a that   b for   c no word

G Complete the sentences

Some of these sentences need a word in the gap to complete them and some don't. Either write one word to complete the sentence or put a dash (–) if you think the sentence doesn't need another word.

1 You can't make the dog _____ go outside on a terrible day like today.

2 We are okay down here, but the actual village _____ itself is often cut off by the snow.

3 I refuse _____ go to the shops until it stops raining.

4 It's getting quite cold so I think I'm going to go to _____ bed.

5 Come in out of the snow and make yourself at _____ home.

6 Lisa came in so wet that it looked _____ if she had been swimming.

7 We were all a little frightened of the storm, even _____ my dad pretended not to be.

8 Eventually, the snow was so deep it reached _____ the kitchen window.

Unit 9

H Find the extra word

One of the words in italics is wrong in each sentence. Circle the word you think should not be there.

1 The man in the shop asked me if there would be anything *else other*.

2 Was there anyone *other else* than you caught in the storm?

3 I hope I never have to go on *one another* trip like that one during the winter.

4 I don't think we need anything else *other apart* from some sun cream.

5 I'm sure there was something *other else* I was supposed to get but I can't remember.

Grammar focus

Read these sentences with relative clauses and choose the best explanation of the meaning of the words in italics. Then, complete the rules by circling the correct option.

1 The River Lee, *which is over fifty miles long*, flooded due to the heavy rain.
a This is just extra information and could be left out.
b This is essential for us to know which river we are talking about.

2 The man *who forecasts the weather on Channel 12* isn't really a meteorologist.
a This is just extra information and could be left out.
b This is essential for us to know which man we are talking about.

3 The storm *that was expected at the weekend* never came.
a This is just extra information and could be left out.
b This is essential for us to know which storm we are talking about.

4 You can see the spot *where a bolt of lightning struck the house* up there.
a This is just extra information and could be left out.
b This is essential for us to know which place we are talking about.

1 We generally use 'who' / 'which' or 'that' when we are talking about people.
2 We generally use 'who' / 'which' or 'that' when we are talking about things.
3 We generally use 'who' / 'where' or 'in which' when we are talking about places.
4 If the relative clause contains extra information, we put / don't put commas around it.
5 If the relative clause is essential for us to know which one we are talking about, we put / don't put commas around it.
6 We use / don't use 'that' in a relative clause which gives extra information and which has commas round it.

EXAM PRACTICE — USE OF ENGLISH PART 4

Exam know-how

When you do Use of English Part 4:
- Remember that they often test words that have two structures, like 'insist that' and 'insist on'. They might put something like 'insist on that …'. Look at these carefully and decide which structure is correct. After you remove a word, read the whole sentence to see if the meaning is appropriate.
- One of the things they are trying to test in this part of the exam is mistakes which First Certificate students often make in their own writing. Study your compositions and the corrections your teacher makes. Learn from your mistakes and look for the same mistakes in Part 4 of the exam.

For questions **1-15**, read the text below and look carefully at each line. Some of the lines are correct, and some have a word which should not be there. If a line is correct, put a tick (✓) by the number. If a line has a word which should **not** be there, write the word on the left. There are two examples at the beginning (**0** and **00**).

Examples:

0	✓
00	on

RAINED OFF

0	✓	A couple of years ago I had a real disappointment. My favourite
00	on	singer, Mariah Carey, was planning to hold on an open-air concert
1	in	in a city near the town in where I live. I was so excited! I was
2	it	the first in the queue for tickets and made it sure that I got a good
3	✓	seat near the front. The concert was being held on Saturday and
4	the	all the week I couldn't think about anything else. I couldn't
5	myself	concentrate myself on my schoolwork and my teachers all said
6	the	that I was daydreaming, but I didn't care. At the last, I was going
7	to	to see Mariah! Friday came and I called to my best friend, Tina,
8	she	who she was going to the concert with me. She answered the
9	that	phone and sounded really unhappy so that I asked her what was
10	✓	wrong. She told me to turn on the TV and watch the weather. I did
11	if	as if she told me and what I saw made my heart sink. The forecast
12	for	for on the weekend was thunderstorms. The concert would have
13	didn't	to be called off if it rained! I hardly didn't sleep at all that night and
14	✓	at three in the morning I heard a loud crack of thunder. The
15	very	forecast had been very right and the concert was cancelled!

Unit 10 The Environment

WARM-UP Pairwork

Look at the pictures. In pairs, ask and answer the following questions:
- What different things can be recycled?
- How much do people recycle things where you live?
- Is enough done in your area to encourage recycling? Why/Why not?

A

B

C

DEVELOP YOUR USE OF ENGLISH SKILLS

What kind of word?

Write what kind of word (nouns, adjectives, verbs, adverbs) can usually be formed using each of the following suffixes. There may be more than one answer for some suffixes. You are given an example after each suffix.

-ness (emptiness) _____
-ise (specialise) _____
-y (delivery, wealthy) _____
-sion (persuasion) _____
-ly (lively, quickly) _____
-less (helpless) _____
-ous (various) _____
-dom (boredom) _____
-ant (inhabitant, reliant) _____
-ful (successful) _____
-ed (bored) _____
-able (reliable) _____

-ity (majority) _____
-al (approval, practical) _____
-ive (passive) _____
-en (tighten, wooden) _____
-ment (amazement) _____
-ary (secondary) _____
-ance (avoidance) _____
-ence (evidence) _____
-tion (operation) _____
-ing (meeting, surprising) _____
-ship (relationship) _____
-ible (responsible) _____

B Discuss (Pairwork)

With your partner, try to think of one more example for each suffix which shows how it is used. Quickly make a list and compare your list with the rest of the class.

C Write the correct noun

All these verbs have nouns ending in '-ment' or '-tion'. For each one, decide which is correct and write the answer in the space provided. You may also have to make other changes to the word. Be careful with your spelling.

achieve	_____	entertain	_____
act	_____	excite	_____
add	_____	explain	_____
agree	_____	improve	_____
amuse	_____	inform	_____
announce	_____	intend	_____
appreciate	_____	invent	_____
argue	_____	investigate	_____
arrange	_____	involve	_____
associate	_____	judge	_____
compete	_____	measure	_____
construct	_____	oblige	_____
converse	_____	observe	_____
decorate	_____	organise	_____
develop	_____	pay	_____
embarrass	_____	prepare	_____
employ	_____	produce	_____
encourage	_____	qualify	_____
enjoy	_____	vary	_____

D Write the correct noun

Each of these words can form nouns which end in '-ance' or '-ence'. Write the correct nouns in the spaces provided.

appear	_____	important	_____
attend	_____	independent	_____
correspond	_____	insist	_____
differ	_____	occur	_____
distant	_____	patient	_____
disturb	_____	perform	_____
evident	_____	refer	_____
exist	_____	resident	_____

Unit 10

DEVELOP YOUR USE OF ENGLISH SKILLS

 Circle the correct noun
Each of the following words can form one of the nouns given. Decide which noun is correct and circle it.

accurate	accuracy / accurence		major	majorness / majority
active	activety / activity		mix	mixment / mixture
anxious	anxiety / anxity		popular	populuation / popularity
deliver	delivery / deliverness		possible	possability / possibility
fit	fitness / fitiency		repeat	repetition / repeation
free	freement / freedom		secure	securement / security
inhabit	inhabitant / inhabitor		tend	tendency / tendancy
know	knowlege / knowledge		vary	variaty / variety
machine	machinity / machinery		willing	willingment / willingness

F Complete the passage
All the words missing are nouns. Write suitable nouns in the gaps formed from the words in bold.

Going green

There is an _____ (**argue**) that _____ (**recycle**) may have some unforeseen negative effects. Of course, it would be a major _____ (**achieve**) if we were able to increase _____ (**aware**) of the threat to the environment caused by _____ (**pollute**) and the _____ (**burn**) of fossil fuels. However, if the public's only _____ (**involve**) in ecological issues is taking their newspapers and bottles to a recycling point, we may only be creating the _____ (**appear**) of _____ (**improve**). If they have to drive any _____ (**distant**) to the recycling point, for example, it might mean the _____ (**consume**) of more energy than is saved. Also, if people feel that they are making their _____ (**contribute**) to the environment, they might not put so much pressure on large _____ (**organise**) to encourage the _____ (**develop**) of safer, less damaging forms of _____ (**produce**).

 Complete the words
Write one letter in each gap to complete the words. Circle the ones that are not people.

contain____r   invent____r   custom____r   research____r

direct____r   freez____r   sail____r   act____r

invest____r   explor____r   inspect____r   protect____r

H Write the adverbs
Write adverbs that can be formed from these words. Be careful with your spelling.

amaze	_____	happy	_____
believe	_____	normal	_____
easy	_____	origin	_____
extreme	_____	recent	_____
general	_____	repeat	_____

I Complete the sentences
Write an appropriate verb in each gap formed from the word in bold. Be careful with your spelling.

1 Schools should _____ (**emphasis**) the importance of looking after the environment.

2 The government should _____ (**tight**) up the rules on river pollution.

3 My uncle is a scientist and he _____ (**special**) in the study of birds and their reactions to pollution.

4 I hope I'll one day be able to _____ (**real**) my dream of becoming a conservationist.

5 We should _____ (**wide**) our idea of our environment and look at the kind of cities we are building.

J Complete the table
Write an appropriate adjective in the correct column(s) for each word. Be careful with your spelling. One of the words has an entry in all three columns.

	-able	-ful	-less
believe	_____	_____	_____
care	_____	_____	_____
comfort	_____	_____	_____
count	_____	_____	_____
desire	_____	_____	_____
end	_____	_____	_____
enjoy	_____	_____	_____
harm	_____	_____	_____
help	_____	_____	_____
hope	_____	_____	_____
power	_____	_____	_____
profit	_____	_____	_____
success	_____	_____	_____
suit	_____	_____	_____
use	_____	_____	_____
value	_____	_____	_____

Unit 10

K Write the suffix

Write an appropriate suffix to complete each adjective in the following sentences.

1 Recycling is a very attract_____ idea but it means investment in services and the money has to come from somewhere.

2 This government has to realise that people are becoming very anx_____ about the pollution in this area.

3 Investing in public transport is a very effect_____ way of reducing the number of cars on the roads.

4 Of course, there are all kinds of practic_____ problems to be faced in dealing with this kind of pollution.

5 The largest problem around here is industr_____ waste produced by local factories.

6 Organic fruit, which has been grown without chemicals, is usually more expens_____ than ordinary fruit.

7 This country has a very impress_____ record of recycling its rubbish.

8 As usual, politic_____ problems mean that the government cannot do anything about the latest environmental disaster.

9 We can only afford to put bottle banks in the town centre if the local council makes addition_____ money available.

10 I get quite depress_____ when I think about the damage we are doing to the environment.

Grammar focus

Choose the correct option to complete these sentences. Then, tick (✓) the sentences a-c which mean the same. You may have to tick more than one sentence in each case.

1 The river near us is too polluted <u>to support / for supporting</u> much life.
a The river contains so much pollution that it cannot support much life.
b Not much life can be supported by the river because there isn't enough pollution.
c It is such a polluted river that it can't support much life.

2 It was such a big oil spill <u>that / so that</u> it caused problems all along the coast.
a The oil spill was big enough to cause problems all along the coast.
b The oil spill was too big to cause problems all along the coast.
c The oil spill was so big that it caused problems all along the coast.

3 There is so much rubbish around here <u>that / so that</u> it's beginning to smell.
a There's such a lot of rubbish around here that it's beginning to smell.
b There's not enough rubbish around here to begin to smell.
c There's too much rubbish around here to begin to smell.

4 There's not enough pollution <u>to cause / for causing</u> serious problems.
a There's too little pollution to cause serious problems.
b There's such little pollution that it doesn't cause serious problems.
c The amount of pollution is so small that it doesn't cause serious problems.

EXAM PRACTICE — USE OF ENGLISH PART 5

Exam know-how

When you do Use of English Part 5:
- Don't forget that the word you have to write could be plural. That might mean that the spelling changes (for example, 'variety' and 'varieties'). Make sure you spell all of your answers correctly.
- If you know what kind of word you need (noun, adjective, etc) but you can't remember exactly the right one, take an educated guess. Use your knowledge of suffixes and prefixes to help you come up with a word that could be correct. Don't leave any gaps blank.

For questions **1-10**, read the text below. Use the word given in capitals at the end of each line to form a word that fits in the space in the same line. There is an example at the beginning (**0**).

Example: | 0 | incredibly |

THE CAR

The car has been (0) ......*incredibly*...... successful. In one century it has come   **INCREDIBLE**
to dominate most of the world and the (1) .... of any developed country   **INHABIT**
rely on it in all kinds of ways. Its (2) .... , though, has had worrying effects   **POPULAR**
on our environment. The (3) .... of roads has meant the destruction of   **CONSTRUCT**
areas of natural beauty. The (4) .... fumes produced by car engines   **HARM**
affect us and the (5) .... species we share the planet with. Scientists and   **COUNT**
other environmental (6) .... are keen to draw attention to the dangers   **SPECIAL**
of our modern lifestyles. However, people seem (7) .... reluctant   **EXTREME**
to give up their cars. Life behind the wheel is too (8) .... and any worries   **COMFORT**
about nature and its problems are (9) .... Unless we can get over our   **SECOND**
attachment to the car, we will face a (10) .... problem of environmental   **GROW**
damage.

Practice Exam 5

Part 1

For questions **1-15**, read the text below and decide which answer (**A, B, C** or **D**) best fits each space. There is an example at the beginning (**0**).

Example:

0   A conceived   B imagined   C considered   D regarded

| 0 | A | B | **C** | D |

THE HANGING GARDENS OF BABYLON

The Hanging Gardens of Babylon were **(0)** ..... to be one of the Seven Wonders of the **(1)** ..... World. They are believed to have been built by King Nebuchadnezzar in the sixth **(2)** ..... BC as a present for his wife, Amytis.

The gardens were **(3)** ..... in layers – one on top of the other, much like a modern multi-storey car **(4)** ....., although a lot more **(5)** ..... to look at. Each layer was a large terrace **(6)** ..... with tropical flowers, plants and trees. The large **(7)** ..... of water which these plants required was **(8)** ..... from the river Euphrates nearby. It is said that Nebuchadnezzar and his wife would sit in the **(9)** ..... of the gardens and **(10)** ..... down on the city of Babylon below.

The gardens' fame quickly **(11)** ....., and travellers would come from far and wide to **(12)** ..... them. Even thousands of years ago, people used to go **(13)** ..... ! The city of Babylon itself was also famous throughout the whole **(14)** ..... for its beautiful buildings, huge tiled walls and magnificent gates made of brass.

Sadly, nothing **(15)** ..... today of the beautiful hanging gardens, and the city of Babylon lies in ruins in what is modern-day Iraq.

1	A Antique	B Ancient	C Historical	D Traditional
2	A decade	B period	C era	D century
3	A constructed	B assembled	C collected	D invented
4	A park	B stop	C station	D garage
5	A good-looking	B attractive	C handsome	D adorable
6	A included	B contained	C filled	D consisted
7	A total	B sum	C amount	D number
8	A dragged	B pulled	C pushed	D pumped
9	A shadow	B shade	C gloom	D glow
10	A look	B see	C watch	D observe
11	A distributed	B spread	C extended	D moved
12	A approve	B respect	C admire	D assess
13	A glimpsing	B sightseeing	C glancing	D staring
14	A planet	B globe	C earth	D world
15	A remains	B stays	C waits	D continues

Part 2

For questions **16-30**, read the text below and think of the word which best fits each space. Use only **one** word in each space. There is an example at the beginning (**0**).

Example: | 0 | its |

THE PIANO

The piano – or, to give it **(0)** ......*its*...... full name, the pianoforte – has played a central role in European music **(16)** .... the early 1700s. Its development can **(17)** .... traced back to an Italian harpsichord maker, Bartolomeo Cristofori.

Cristofori **(18)** .... wanted for a long time to combine the mechanisms of two different instruments: the dulcimer, which relies **(19)** .... strings and hammers to produce its sound, and the harpsichord, **(20)** .... music is produced through a keyboard.

In 1709 Cristofori worked out **(21)** .... this could be done successfully, and the piano **(22)** .... born. The piano player strikes a key on the keyboard, **(23)** .... forces a hammer to strike a string, producing a note. The idea seems obvious **(24)** .... us today, but in 1709 it was revolutionary.

The piano quickly **(25)** .... extremely popular, and improvements continued to be **(26)** .... to it. Foot pedals were introduced **(27)** .... the end of the eighteenth century.

Although pianos have been made in a wide variety **(28)** .... different shapes and sizes, today **(29)** .... are really only two main types of piano, the Grand **(30)** .... the Upright.

Part 3

For questions **31-40**, complete the second sentence so that it has a similar meaning to the first sentence, using the word given. **Do not change the word given.** You must use between **two** and **five** words, including the word given. Here is an example (**0**).

Example:

0 You must do exactly what the manager tells you.
carry
You must .... instructions exactly.

The gap can be filled by the words 'carry out the manager's' so you write:

0	carry out the manager's

---

31 Cricket doesn't interest Bill.
interested
Bill .... cricket.

32 I expect you were very pleased when you won the competition.
been
You .... very pleased when you won the competition.

33 This packet is completely empty.
left
There's .... this packet.

34 My house is quite near the train station.
far
My house .... the train station.

35 I'd love to come to your wedding, but I'll be away on holiday then.
wish
I .... to your wedding, but I'll be away on holiday then.

36 Tim should learn how to cook now.
time
It's .... how to cook.

37 Reports suggest that the criminals are hiding in an abandoned building.
thought
The criminals .... in an abandoned building.

38 The switchboard operator connected me to the complaints department.
put
The switchboard operator .... the complaints department.

39 No one disagreed with the idea apart from Melissa.
exception
With .... , everyone agreed with the idea.

40 Alan does a full-time job and brings up two children too.
well
Alan does a full-time job .... two children.

Part 4

For questions **41-55**, read the text below and look carefully at each line. Some of the lines are correct, and some have a word which should not be there. If a line is correct, put a tick (✓) by the number. If a line has a word which should **not** be there, write the word on the left. There are two examples at the beginning (**0** and **00**).

Examples:

0	✓
00	up

THE SURPRISE PARTY

0	✓	Last Friday was my dad's birthday, and we organised a surprise
00	up	party for him. It was great! We decorated up the living room with
41	was	balloons and Mum was baked a big cake. There were forty
42	of	candles on the cake because of my dad was forty years old.
43	✓	We invited all the family and lots of his friends, and waited in the
44	the	living room for him to come home from the work. It was very
45	there	funny! We had turned out all the lights, and there were hiding
46	the	behind the chairs, the sofa and the curtains. As the usual, he
47	✓	came into the house and shouted 'Hi, everyone! I'm home!' We
48	out	didn't make out a sound. 'Where is everyone?' he said, and
49	did	came into the room. He turned on the lights and we all did
50	of	shouted 'Surprise!'. He was so shocked! Dad blew out of all the
51	to	candles on the cake and we sang 'Happy Birthday'. I gave to him
52	✓	a tie and my brother got him a CD. Mum bought him a bottle of
53	have	his favourite wine. We have had a great party, and Dad said it
54	✓	was the best birthday he had ever had. He also said that for
55	as	being forty wasn't as too bad as he had thought it would be.

Part 5

For questions **56-65**, read the text below. Use the word given in capitals at the end of each line to form a word that fits in the space in the same line. There is an example at the beginning (**0**).

Example: | 0 | unbelievable |

THE END OF THE SECRETARY

It may seem **(0)** ....unbelievable...., but it is quite possible that the days of the secretary are coming to an end. There is **(56)** .... to suggest that professional people such as doctors, **(57)** .... and managers are dealing with **(58)** .... personally rather than having a secretary do it. And the reason is simple: modern technology.

BELIEVE
EVIDENT
LAW
CORRESPOND

Until recently, secretaries were extremely **(59)** .... for typing letters to **(60)** .... and clients, for arranging meetings and dealing with travel **(61)** .... Answering the telephone was also another of their major **(62)** .... However, with the introduction of e-mail and mobile phones, managers are able to do more and more of these **(63)** .... themselves. Many companies **(64)** .... have fewer secretaries than they did five years ago. However, **(65)** .... does not seem to have increased as a result. Rather, secretaries are finding new positions as personal assistants and even managers themselves.

USE
CUSTOM
ARRANGE
RESPONSIBLE
ACTIVE
CURRENT
EMPLOY

Unit 11 Technology

WARM-UP

Look at the picture.
In pairs, ask and answer the following questions:
- What does the word 'technology' make you think of?
- Are there other things that we might think of as 'technology'?
- Was discovering how to make fires an important technological development?

DEVELOP YOUR USE OF ENGLISH SKILLS

A Choose the correct answer
Circle the word or phrase which best completes each of the following sentences.

1 Technology will probably continue to develop _____ we think that is a good thing for our society or not.
   a whether   **b** although   **c** despite

2 We have to be careful with the technology we develop, _____ we could find ourselves facing serious environmental problems.
   a although   **b** whereas   **c** otherwise

3 It's far too late for us to be able to live without computers again, _____ we wanted to.
   a despite   **b** even if   **c** although

4 Today, we build machines to do heavy or dangerous work for us, _____ primitive people had to rely on their own skill and courage.
   a otherwise   **b** no matter   **c** whereas

5 Technology means that many people now work from home, _____ there will probably always be a need for offices.
   a although   **b** however   **c** otherwise

6 Poorer countries will remain poor _____ we enable them to develop technological skills.
   a despite   **b** regardless of **c** unless

7 McDougal's are thinking of introducing a new computer system, even _____ that means that some people will lose their jobs.
   a although   **b** since   **c** if

86

8 I've saved all my pocket money for two months and it's _____ not enough to buy that new computer game.
   a even   b still   c however

9 The latest game from Megasoft is a great adventure story, _____ a little violent for some people.
   a even   b if   c whether

10 My dad always has to have the latest piece of technology, _____ how much it costs.
   a in spite   b no matter   c even though

B Complete the passage
Complete the following passage by circling the correct words.

Because / In spite of computers and other inventions, it is easy for us to think of 'technology' as something recent. Although / However it's true that we rely on machines more than ever before, technology has always been a part of human life. Fire and the wheel were important advances, even if / as we think of them as simple today. Our ancient ancestors also created stone axes, no matter / otherwise they wouldn't have been able to hunt effectively. Later, people discovered metal, though / despite plastics were not discovered until modern times. We have to realise that our whole history is the history of technology, regardless of / nevertheless the exact form it took.

C Complete the sentences
Use the words in the box to complete the sentences.

    better   rather   further

1 Instead of building more computers, I think the money would be _____ spent on fighting social problems.

2 The government are considering banning _____ research into genetic engineering.

3 I thought you said you'd _____ have a new telescope for your birthday and now you say you want a computer.

4 If you want to be a computer programmer, you'd _____ find out what kind of training you need to do.

5 Don't you think you should do some exercise, _____ than sitting and playing computer games all the time?

6 Please contact our customer helpline if you require _____ information on setting up your new P9000 computer.

Unit 11

DEVELOP YOUR USE OF ENGLISH SKILLS

D Choose the correct answer
Circle the correct word to complete the following sentences.

1. Technological progress seems to happen _____ quickly for us to keep up.
   a so   b such   c enough   d too

2. There are _____ few good games for the Playmaster that I don't think I'm going to bother getting one.
   a so   b such   c enough   d too

3. We've had _____ problems with our new computer that we had to send it back to the shop.
   a so   b such   c enough   d too

4. I've had _____ trouble with my car to make me think twice about getting another Mercedes.
   a so   b such   c enough   d too

5. I'm afraid we no longer sell that model of laptop because we had _____ a lot of complaints.
   a so   b such   c enough   d too

E Complete the passage
Use the words in the box to complete the passage. Use each word only once.

> better   so   enough   rather   such   further   too

IT'S HERE, AND IT'S COOL!

Ultracon, the latest games console from Sonatendo is (1)_____ cool it'll blow your mind! It arrived in this country last week and everyone wants one. It's got (2)_____ good graphics your eyes will think they've suddenly woken up! It's got (3)_____ power to run all the latest games, from *Freak Force VI* to *Underworld Soccer*, without even breaking into a sweat! If you think your time can be (4)_____ spent, then prepare to think again. The Ultracon is almost (5)_____ good for us to describe. I'd (6)_____ play football on this machine than do the real thing! It's that good! Put it on your birthday list and your Christmas list and watch out for (7)_____ developments from the guys at Sonatendo.

F Circle the correct word
Circle the correct word to complete each of the following sentences.

1 There are still / just / yet a great number of technological challenges which we face.
2 There are yet / just / already a number of people around the world working to invent a practical electric engine.
3 There are just / even / yet a few decades left before we find ourselves dealing with artificial intelligence.
4 I still / yet / already can't get to level five until I kill the monster at the end of level four.
5 Richard invented a new way of producing energy while then / still / already at university.

G Choose the correct verb
Circle the correct verb to complete each sentence.

1 As soon as I have _____ the car cleaned, I'll drive you to your computer lesson.
   a done   b made   c had
2 Please don't put me on hold – I have already _____ waiting for fifteen minutes.
   a been   b done   c had
3 Actually, Martha wrote this computer programme, but I _____ give her some help.
   a was   b did   c have
4 You _____ supposed to do your computing homework, not surf the internet!
   a had   b did   c were
5 I've been trying to fix the washing machine all morning and now I'm _____ rather annoyed with it.
   a having   b getting   c being

H Match to make sentences
Match the sentence beginnings on the left with their endings on the right.

1 I don't really like computers, even _____
2 We've got a computer but, even _____
3 My sister loves computer games, even _____
4 I probably do play on my computer a lot, even _____
5 My mum doesn't visit websites, even _____

a those with a lot of violence and fast action.
b though I know I'll have to use them in the future.
c so, I don't know the first thing about using it.
d when I should be doing other things.
e if I find ones that I think might interest her.

Unit 11

1 Circle the correct word

Circle the correct word to complete the following sentences.

1 All computer games interest me, except _____ that are supposed to be educational.
   a they   **b** those   **c** which

2 May and Nadine wanted to use your CD player so I let _____ borrow it.
   a them   **b** those   **c** they

3 The internet means more freedom for people who understand it, but might be a problem for _____ people who don't.
   a those   **b** they   **c** which

4 There are _____ who believe that we will eventually create a computer that can think.
   a these   **b** some   **c** them

5 They've got a good selection of computer games here, but I'm really looking for _____ with less violence in them.
   a they   **b** them   **c** ones

Grammar focus

Circle the letters to complete the following sentences. There may be more than one correct choice.

Talking about a general truth
If you heat water …
a   it boils at one hundred degrees centigrade.
b   it will boil at one hundred degrees centigrade.
c   it would boil at one hundred degrees centigrade.

Talking about a real possibility in the present or future
If I have some time this evening …
a   I'll read my computer magazine.
b   I would have read my computer magazine.
c   I'm going to read my computer magazine.

Should I find your palmtop …
a   I'll bring it round to your house.
b   I would have brought it round to your house.
c   I had brought it round to your house.

Talking about an unlikely or impossible situation in the present or future
If I had more money …
a   I will buy myself a new computer.
b   I would buy myself a new computer.
c   I had myself a new computer.

Were we to buy a computer …
a   I'd be able to write e-mails to friends.
b   I would have sent more e-mails.
c   we could learn something about the internet.

Talking about something which did not happen in the past
If I had paid more attention in science lessons …
a   I could have studied physics at university.
b   I would probably be a scientist now.
c   I will study physics at university.

Had I known how useful mobile phones were …
a   I had got one a long time ago.
b   I would have got one a long time ago.
c   I'll get one as soon as possible.

Exam practice — Use of English part 1

Exam know-how

When you do Use of English Part 1:
- Remember to look at the whole sentence carefully so that you know whether a word fits into the gap grammatically.
- Pay attention to connecting words and phrases, such as 'although' and 'otherwise'. Learn what each one means and how it is used.

For questions **1-15**, read the text below and decide which answer (**A, B, C or D**) best fits each space. There is an example at the beginning (**0**).

Example:

0   **A** existing   **B** surviving   **C** living   **D** being   0 A **B** C D

THE ORIGINS OF PHOTOGRAPHY

The world's first (0) ..... photograph was taken in 1827 by a Frenchman called Niepce. Up to that (1) ..... , it had been impossible to capture permanently a living image, (2) ..... in a painting or drawing. Niepce pointed his early camera at the window of his country home and produced an image. It wasn't very (3) ..... , and it took him eight hours in bright sunlight, but the image still survives to this day.
Another Frenchman, Daguerre, heard about Niepce's work and (4) ..... him. They became (5) ..... and worked together to create a new photographic process. This process was very complicated and (6) ..... a great deal of skill. (7) ..... the difficulties, it became very popular and soon people around the world were taking daguerreotypes, as they were known. In England, William Henry Fox Talbot (8) ..... developed his own process at about the same time that Daguerre and Niepce were working on theirs. His method (9) ..... more than one copy to be made, (10) ..... the daguerreotype could not be reproduced.
This new technology created all kinds of opportunities for (11) ..... brave enough to travel to remote locations and to go into dangerous situations. Photographers (12) ..... as Roger Fenton of England and Matthew Brady of America took some of the first war photographs.
By the 1880s, (13) ..... American George Eastman produced the first Kodak camera, the world was ready for mass photography. The Kodak camera had a roll of film inside and was (14) ..... easier to use than any previous camera. It was an instant success and soon people were (15) ..... their picture taken as if it were the most ordinary thing in the world.

1	**A** point	**B** period	**C** occasion	**D** mark
2	**A** although	**B** except	**C** despite	**D** otherwise
3	**A** clean	**B** shiny	**C** smooth	**D** clear
4	**A** contacted	**B** communicated	**C** informed	**D** greeted
5	**A** companions	**B** partners	**C** rivals	**D** opponents
6	**A** claimed	**B** demanded	**C** asked	**D** mentioned
7	**A** In spite	**B** Though	**C** However	**D** Despite
8	**A** had	**B** was	**C** did	**D** got
9	**A** made	**B** allowed	**C** let	**D** produced
10	**A** yet	**B** even	**C** whereas	**D** otherwise
11	**A** those	**B** some	**C** they	**D** ones
12	**A** even	**B** so	**C** just	**D** such
13	**A** where	**B** when	**C** which	**D** while
14	**A** considerably	**B** extremely	**C** absolutely	**D** completely
15	**A** being	**B** having	**C** doing	**D** making

Unit 12 Health and Fitness

WARM-UP *Pairwork*

Look at the pictures. In pairs, ask and answer the following questions:
- What do you know about these alternative forms of treatment?
- Do you think Western medicine can learn anything from alternative medicine?
- Would you consider trying any of these forms of treatment if you were ill?

A

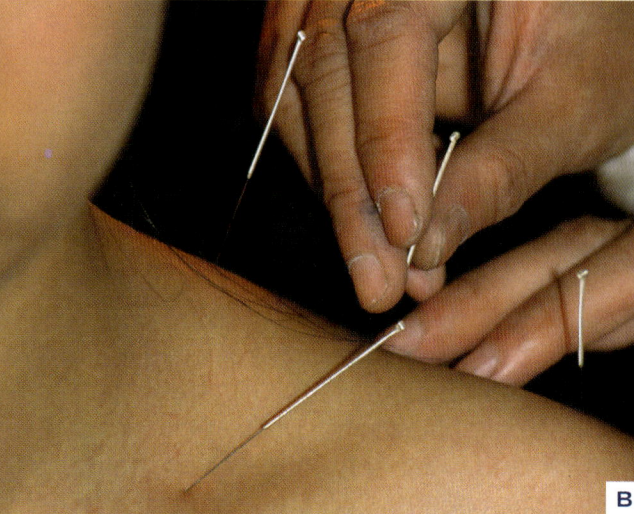
B

DEVELOP YOUR USE OF ENGLISH SKILLS

A Make or do?

Decide whether these phrases go with the verbs 'make' or 'do'. Write **make** or **do** on the lines provided.

_____ an appointment
_____ the best of something
_____ a complaint
_____ a difference
_____ an exercise
_____ fun of someone
_____ the housework
_____ a meal
_____ a noise
_____ sense
_____ someone do something
_____ up your mind
_____ an arrangement
_____ your best
_____ the cooking

_____ a drink
_____ an experiment
_____ a fuss
_____ homework
_____ a mess
_____ a phone call
_____ the shopping
_____ a suggestion
_____ the washing-up
_____ the bed
_____ certain
_____ damage
_____ your duty
_____ friends
_____ good

_____ the ironing
_____ a mistake
_____ a plan
_____ some work
_____ sure
_____ well
_____ a decision
_____ an effort
_____ a fortune
_____ you good
_____ a job
_____ money
_____ research
_____ someone a favour

B Have or take?

For each set of words and phrases, choose the odd one out. For example, we say 'take place' not 'have place', so 'place' is the odd one out.

Example:

have ...	a party	[place]	a good time	a meal
1 **have ...**	a plan	an idea	an interview	a decision
2 **have ...**	an argument	a lesson	pity on someone	a family
3 **have ...**	an effect	a chance to do something	a nice time	the blame
4 **take ...**	difficulty	care	turns	part in something
5 **take ...**	something into account	advantage of something	to do something	pleasure in something

C Have, or have and take?

Some of these words and phrases only go with the verb 'have'. Others go with both 'have' and 'take'. Write **have** or **have/take** on the lines provided.

1 _____ a bath
2 _____ a break
3 _____ a day off
4 _____ a dream
5 _____ a hair wash
6 _____ a holiday
7 _____ a job
8 _____ a look at something
9 _____ a nightmare
10 _____ a shower
11 _____ an exam
12 _____ an experience
13 _____ qualifications
14 _____ something to do
15 _____ time to do something
16 _____ a role/part to play

D Discuss

Some of the phrases above that can go with 'have' and 'take' have different meanings depending on which verb is used. Discuss what the differences in meaning are.

Unit 12

DEVELOP YOUR USE OF ENGLISH SKILLS

E Complete the passage
Use the verbs **make**, **do**, **have** and **take** in their correct forms to complete this passage.

Getting fit!
June Bishop decides to get in shape.

Last week, I (1)_____ an important decision. I decided to get fit. Until recently, I just haven't (2)_____ time to go to a gym. I work full-time in a busy office, and I (3)_____ a large family, so when I'm not at work, I'm (4)_____ the shopping, (5)_____ the beds, (6)_____ the ironing, (7)_____ dinner, clearing up all the mess that the kids have (8)_____ and generally (9)_____ all the housework. So, I'm busy and active, but not particularly fit.

But with the kids away at summer camp for a few weeks, I realised that I (10)_____ the perfect chance to (11)_____ something about it. I immediately (12)_____ advantage of the peace and quiet, and (13)_____ an appointment with a personal trainer at a local gym.

It was great! I'd (14)_____ the idea that all these really fit body-builders would (15)_____ fun of me, but in fact the atmosphere was very relaxed and friendly. My personal trainer – Tony – encouraged me to (16)_____ my best, although he warned me to (17)_____ care not to overdo things in the first session. He wanted to (18)_____ sure I didn't injure myself. At the end of the hour, he said I'd (19)_____ very well.

I've been to the gym four times now, and I'm extremely glad I (20)_____ the effort. Exercise clearly (21)_____ you good, and my workouts have (22)_____ an effect already. I feel a lot healthier. It's really (23)_____ a difference. And I've also (24)_____ some good friends there. I've (25)_____ up my mind to continue, even when the kids come back.

Whenever I have a day off, usually every Tuesday, I'm going to (26)_____ the best of the little free time I (27)_____, head off to the gym and (28)_____ some exercise. I know it (29)_____ sense, I (30)_____ a great time whenever I go there and it's (31)_____ me realise that there's more to life than just work.

94

F Phrasal verbs

Circle the correct words to complete these sentences.

1 The doctor says he wants you to **carry** on / out / off taking these pills for at least two weeks.
2 Don't forget to **put** those tablets away / down / off before the kids come round. We don't want them eating them by mistake.
3 Mrs Jenkins was too ill to go out and pay her phone bill, and they've just **cut** her out / off / down. She ought to complain!
4 Dawn's thinking of **setting** out / in / up a social club for local disabled people.
5 The corner shop had **sold** off / out / up of / from aspirin, so I had to go to the chemist.
6 I wish someone would **come** down / up / off with / to an easy and simple way for me to quit smoking.
7 Our cat's nearly sixteen now, and I'm really worried the vet's going to say we ought to **put** him out / down / away.
8 The holiday was a disaster! I **came** down / up / in with / to food poisoning on the first day and spent the whole time in bed.
9 I wish the politicians would **sort** out / up / through the problem of hospital waiting lists. My grandmother had to wait over a year for her operation.
10 I'm so glad to hear you've **got** up / out of / over your illness. It must have been awful being stuck at home for so long.

G Take place, happen and occur

These three verbs have very similar meanings and can sometimes be used synonymously. Sometimes, however, they cannot.
First, write **take place**, **happen** or **occur** in these gaps to complete these descriptions.

1 We can use '_____' as a more formal synonym for **happen** in sentences such as: 'Luckily, he was in hospital when his heart attack happened.'
2 We can use '_____' to mean **exist**.
3 When '_____' is followed by 'to someone' it means **affect someone** or **be experienced by someone**.
4 When '_____' is followed by 'to someone' it means **suddenly realise**.
5 We usually use '_____' for organised, planned or controlled events.

Now, circle the best verb to complete each sentence. Then write it in the correct tense and person on the line provided.

1 Aerobics classes are scheduled to (take place / occur) _____ in the Community Centre every Thursday at eight o'clock.
2 The disease (happen / occur) _____ more frequently in elderly patients.
3 Didn't it (take place / occur) _____ to you to call an ambulance?
4 Losing weight is the best thing that ever (happen / occur) _____ to me.
5 I wonder what will (take place / happen) _____ if they prove that mobile phones are really dangerous. Will people stop using them?

Unit 12

H **Complete the passage**
Write one word in each gap to complete the following passage.

I set (1)_____ The Laughter Clinic in 1999. I (2)_____ up with the idea while I was ill. I'd come (3)_____ with a virus and I was feeling miserable. I was watching TV, and a comedy came on, and I suddenly felt better. It (4)_____ to me that laughter really is the best medicine and I thought, 'Wouldn't it be great to have a clinic where the treatment was humour?' I watched a lot of comedies and I carried (5)_____ getting better. I was sure laughter (6)_____ a part to play in my recovery. When I was better, I (7)_____ some research and found a scientific study which shows that patients who laugh a lot get (8)_____ their illnesses more quickly. Scientists aren't sure why it (9)_____, but it does. Laughter sessions take (10)_____ every morning at our centre in Bristol. If you're feeling ill, or just stressed with trying to (11)_____ out all of life's problems, then come along and (12)_____ part. We'll put the smile back on your face!

Grammar focus

Each of these sentences in the passive voice contains a mistake. Rewrite the words in bold so that the sentence is correct.

1	Physiotherapy sessions **are holding** every Tuesday and Thursday.	present simple
2	Dan **is been treated** by a top physician at the moment.	present continuous
3	Acupuncture **has used** for over 400 years.	present perfect simple
4	Julie **has hypnotised** in an attempt to quit smoking.	past simple
5	I **was being showed** how to use the exercise bike when I tripped over and broke my ankle.	past continuous
6	I knew I **have been prescribed** some medicine but I didn't know what it was for.	past perfect
7	You **will be being informed** what time your appointment is at a later date.	future simple
8	We are **going to given** flu jabs at school tomorrow.	'going to'
9	This time next week my plaster **will been cut off**.	future perfect
10	My plaster will be cut off **from** a nurse.	agent
11	It will be cut off **by** a special saw which doesn't cut skin.	instrument

EXAM PRACTICE — USE OF ENGLISH PART 2

Exam know-how

When you do Use of English Part 2:
- Although most of the gaps are designed to test your grammar, remember that a few of them will test your vocabulary. Often, these test set phrases such as 'make sure' or 'take advantage of'. Make sure you learn as many of these phrases as possible before the exam.
- Remember that phrasal verbs are also sometimes tested in this part. If there is a gap before a word like 'up', 'in' or 'on', or if there is a gap after a verb, always ask yourself if a phrasal verb is required.

For questions **1-15**, read the text below and think of the word which best fits each space. Use only **one** word in each space. There is an example at the beginning (**0**).

Example: | 0 | which |

ACUPUNCTURE

Acupuncture is a Chinese medical technique **(0)** ......*which*...... has been practised for **(1)** .... than 4000 years. It involves inserting long thin needles into particular spots in the skin, **(2)** .... as acupuncture points, and rotating them. It is mainly used **(3)** .... relieve pain but it is also sometimes used for curing disease and improving general health.

Acupuncture is **(4)** .... of the great mysteries of medical science. **(5)** .... is little doubt that it can be effective in relieving pain. Western doctors have witnessed surgical operations carried **(6)** .... on Chinese patients who were anaesthetised only by acupuncture and yet showed no signs **(7)** .... pain. However, Western scientists have still not **(8)** .... up with an adequate explanation as to how acupuncture actually works. At one time it was believed that acupuncture was related in some way to hypnosis, but this has now been proved **(9)** .... to be true. Still, acupuncture is **(10)** .... increasingly popular here in the West, with many American and European doctors now believing acupuncture may **(11)** .... a role to play in medicine, although most argue that much more research needs to be **(12)** .... first.

In 1972, acupuncture received some welcome publicity **(13)** .... a result of President Nixon's trip to China. Nixon became ill during the trip and **(14)** .... rushed to hospital. He later **(15)** .... reporters that acupuncture had greatly relieved his pain.

Practice Exam 6

Part 1

For questions **1-15**, read the text below and decide which answer (**A**, **B**, **C** or **D**) best fits each space. There is an example at the beginning (**0**).

Example:

0   **A** noticed   **B** conceived   **C** invented   **D** found

0	A	B	**C**	D

TELEVISION

If you ask anyone who **(0)** ..... television, they will tell you that it was John Logie Baird. While Baird was, of course, extremely important in the history of television, it would be more **(1)** ..... to see his role as part of a **(2)** ..... of events which finally led to television as we **(3)** ..... it today.

The history of television really begins in 1817 with the **(4)** ..... by Berzelius, a Swedish chemist, of the chemical selenium. It was found that the amount of electric current that selenium could carry **(5)** ..... on how much light struck it.

This discovery directly led to G. R. Carey, an American inventor, **(6)** ..... up with the first real television system in 1875. His system used selenium to transmit a picture along wires to a **(7)** ..... of light bulbs. This picture was not very clear, however.

Over the next few years, a number of scientists and inventors simplified and **(8)** ..... on Carey's system. It was not **(9)** ..... 1923 that Baird made the first practical transmission. Once again, the picture was **(10)** ..... through wires, but it was much clearer than Carey's had been almost fifty years **(11)** ..... .

The Second World War **(12)** ..... the development of television. After the war, television **(13)** ..... began to flood the market, with the first mass TV **(14)** ..... watching the baseball World Series in the USA in 1947. Within a few years, television had captured the **(15)** ..... of the whole world.

1	**A** particular	**B** accurate	**C** specific	**D** real
2	**A** connection	**B** cycle	**C** link	**D** chain
3	**A** know	**B** realise	**C** comprehend	**D** distinguish
4	**A** discovery	**B** finding	**C** location	**D** sighting
5	**A** resulted	**B** affected	**C** depended	**D** relied
6	**A** going	**B** making	**C** coming	**D** doing
7	**A** procession	**B** list	**C** queue	**D** row
8	**A** bettered	**B** improved	**C** developed	**D** extended
9	**A** until	**B** after	**C** up to	**D** then
10	**A** pushed	**B** sent	**C** transferred	**D** transported
11	**A** ago	**B** before	**C** after	**D** later
12	**A** abandoned	**B** cancelled	**C** delayed	**D** waited
13	**A** sets	**B** boxes	**C** machines	**D** models
14	**A** assembly	**B** audience	**C** gathering	**D** group
15	**A** observation	**B** awareness	**C** notice	**D** attention

Part 2

For questions **16-30**, read the text below and think of the word which best fits each space. Use only **one** word in each space. There is an example at the beginning (**0**).

Example: | 0 | which |

THE COELACANTH

The fish the coelacanth, (0) ....*which*.... was very common during the early history of the world, gets (16) .... name from the Ancient Greek term for 'hollow spine'. At the beginning (17) .... the twentieth century, scientists believed (18) .... the coelacanth was extinct. Indeed, they had worked (19) .... from fossils of coelacanths that it (20) .... been extinct for over sixty million years.

Then, in 1938, an extremely exciting scientific discovery was (21) .... A fisherman fishing off (22) .... coast of South Africa caught a very peculiar fish. He brought it back to the mainland (23) .... analysis, and it was identified from its hollow spine and the shape of its fins (24) .... a coelacanth. The fish was not extinct after (25) .... !

Unfortunately, the fish decomposed rapidly, preventing scientists (26) .... carrying out further studies on it. However, (27) .... 1952 a number of coelacanths have (28) .... caught in the seas around east Africa, (29) .... scientists to examine the fish which everyone had presumed had died (30) .... with the dinosaurs.

Part 3

For questions **31-40**, complete the second sentence so that it has a similar meaning to the first sentence, using the word given. **Do not change the word given**. You must use between **two** and **five** words, including the word given. There is an example at the beginning (**0**).

Example:

0   You must do exactly what the manager tells you.
carry
You must .... instructions exactly.

The gap can be filled by the words 'carry out the manager's' so you write:

0	carry out the manager's

---

31   The teacher advised the class to use a dictionary.
you
'If I .... a dictionary,' said the teacher to the class.

32   My grandmother was sixty when she learnt to drive.
age
My grandmother learnt to drive .... sixty.

33   Bad weather caused the ferry to be delayed.
result
The ferry was delayed .... bad weather.

34   'You've broken my CD player, Darren,' said Fiona.
accused
Fiona .... her CD player.

35   It might rain later so take an umbrella.
case
Take an umbrella .... later.

36   Is it all right for me to make a phone call?
if
Do .... a phone call?

37   Someone is coming to paint our house tomorrow.
painted
We are going .... tomorrow.

38   Helen often gets angry for no reason at all.
tendency
Helen .... angry for no reason at all.

39   Could I stay with you for the weekend?
put
Could you .... for the weekend?

40   Ed did not need to register for the new course.
necessary
It .... to register for the new course.

Part 4

LETTER TO A PEN FRIEND

0	✓	I can't wait until next Thursday. We're going to have such a
00	up	fantastic time! I'll meet up you at the station and we'll get the
41	that	bus to my house. It's not far, so that it won't take long. After you
42	✓	have met my parents, we'll go down to the beach. All my friends
43	so	are going to be there. I think so you'll really like them. Dave, my
44	of	best of friend, is organising a barbecue so we'll eat burgers and
45	in	things by the sea. You mustn't forget to bring in your swimming
46	for	costume because we'll definitely be going for swimming. I think
47	✓	Angela's also going to be bringing her CD player, so it'll be a
48	a	really good beach party. Does that sound a fun? I thought that
49	we	the next day we could go into town and we do some shopping.
50	say	You said you wanted to get some souvenirs, didn't you say?
51	✓	Then, in the evening, we can go to the cinema if there's anything
52	it	good on it. If there isn't, I'll take you to the youth club where
53	less	they're having a disco. I can't believe it's only a few less days
54	to	until we actually meet! I'll call to you on Wednesday evening to
55	that	find out that for sure what time your train gets in on Thursday.

Part 5

CELEBRITIES AND THE MEDIA

It is a (0) ...generally... accepted truth these days that it is impossible either — **GENERAL**
to become or to remain (56) .... without the help of the media. — **FAME**
Politicians and those who work in the (57) .... industry make use of — **ENTERTAIN**
the press to court publicity, and (58) .... are extremely aware that — **JOURNAL**
stories about celebrities sell newspapers.
However, there are (59) .... concerns that the media is abusing its — **GROW**
position, and that it all too frequently acts (60) .... in its attempts — **REASONABLE**
to break a story. Remember the (61) .... on motorbikes chasing — **PHOTO**
Diana through Paris on the night she died? Was that (62) .... — **ACCEPT**
behaviour or were they quite within their rights to act as they did?
The media clearly does have an extremely (63) .... role to play, but — **VALUE**
should it be allowed to print (64) .... and unresearched stories — **ACCURATE**
about celebrities? Surely the media has an (65) .... to respect — **OBLIGE**
the privacy of everyone and print the truth.

Unit 13 Transport

WARM-UP Pairwork

Look at the picture.
In pairs, ask and answer the following questions:
- Should people have to wear seat belts in cars? Why/Why not?
- What do people have to do in the driving test in your country?
- Why do we have speed limits?
- Do you think speed limits in your country should be increased? Why/Why not?

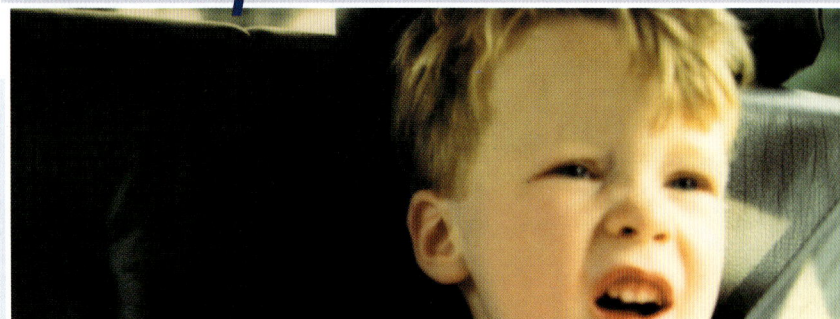

DEVELOP YOUR USE OF ENGLISH SKILLS

A Ability

Decide whether each sentence is correct or not. If it's correct, put a tick (). If it's incorrect, rewrite it correctly.

1. Tanya drives very well. _____
2. Tanya is very good in driving. _____
3. Darren was unable to catch the ferry. _____
4. Darren didn't succeed to catch the ferry. _____
5. Darren didn't manage catching the ferry. _____
6. Darren failed to catch the ferry. _____
7. Bob isn't really capable to sail in rough weather. _____
8. It's impossible for me getting there by four o'clock. _____
9. Can you pick up the tickets for me? _____
10. She wants to know if can I pick up the tickets for her. _____
11. It's difficult to learn how to fly a plane. _____
12. Learning how to fly a plane is difficult. _____
13. James had difficulty to land the plane. _____
14. James found it difficult to land the plane. _____

B Chance and probability

Complete each of the following sentences using the patterns and the key words given. You may need to write more than five words to complete each gap.

1. I'm totally convinced that the airport is closed today.
   chance [there is a/some/no chance of someone/something doing something]
   There _____ open today.

102

2 Ed's instructor says he definitely won't pass his driving test tomorrow.
chance [someone has a/some/no chance of doing something]
Ed's instructor says he _____ his driving test tomorrow.

3 There probably aren't any parking spaces in the car park.
unlikely [it is (un)likely (that) + subject + verb]
It _____ any parking spaces in the car park.

4 Colin probably won't arrive before six o'clock.
unlikely [someone is (un)likely to do something]
Colin _____ before six o'clock.

5 The tickets are bound to be more expensive next month.
doubt [there is some/no doubt (that) + subject + verb]
There _____ expensive next month.

C Responsibility

Circle the correct words to complete these patterns.

1 It is someone's responsibility for doing / to do something.
2 Someone has responsibility for doing / to do something.
3 Someone is responsible for doing / to do something.
4 It is someone's duty for doing / to do something.

Complete these sentences using the words in bold so that they mean the same as this sentence:

Kevin's job on the ferry is to check people's tickets before they set sail.

1 **responsibility**
It _____ people's tickets before the ferry sets sail.

2 **responsibility**
Kevin _____ people's tickets before the ferry sets sail.

3 **responsible**
Kevin _____ people's tickets before the ferry sets sail.

4 **duty**
It _____ people's tickets before the ferry sets sail.

Unit 13

DEVELOP YOUR USE OF ENGLISH SKILLS

D Preference and regret
Complete the sentences so that they mean the same as the sentences given.

1 I don't want to take the bus today.
   I don't feel _____.
   I'd rather _____.

2 Natalie said she wanted to learn how to skateboard.
   Natalie said she would _____.
   Natalie expressed an interest _____.

3 Marcus would really like to be able to hang-glide.
   Marcus wishes he was _____.
   Marcus wishes he could _____.
   Marcus regrets not _____.

4 'Why didn't I learn how to hang-glide before?' wondered Marcus.
   Marcus wondered _____.

5 Tony regrets crashing his mother's Porsche.
   Tony wishes _____.

6 'I'm sorry I didn't drive more carefully,' said Tony.
   Tony wished _____.
   Tony apologised for _____.

E Force, permission and recommendation
Decide whether these patterns are correct or not. If they are correct, put a tick (✓). If they are incorrect, rewrite them correctly.

1 let someone to do something
2 allow someone to do something
3 be let to do something
4 make someone to do something
5 force someone to do something
6 have to do something
7 would advise someone doing something
8 had better to do something
9 be a waste of time for someone to do something
10 be no point at doing something
11 see the point to do something
12 be worth to do something
13 be all right for someone to do something
14 mind if someone does something
15 it is (high) time someone does something
16 give someone permission for doing something

F Complete the sentences

Complete the sentences using the key words given. You must write between two and five words in each gap.

1 Uncle John didn't let me borrow his motorboat. **allowed**
   I _____ Uncle John's motorboat.

2 I'd strongly advise you to wear a life jacket. **better**
   You _____ a life jacket.

3 I'd strongly advise you to put on your seat belt. **you**
   If I _____ put on my seat belt.

4 It's a waste of time for you to get the train tickets in advance. **point**
   There _____ the train tickets in advance.

5 It's a waste of time to get the train tickets in advance. **point**
   I don't _____ the train tickets in advance.

6 You should learn to drive. **time**
   It's _____ to drive.

7 Our neighbours said we could use their caravan while they're away. **permission**
   Our neighbours _____ their caravan while they're away.

G Time and regularity

There is a mistake in each of the second sentences. Rewrite them correctly.

1 How long was the flight from London to Athens?
   How long did it spend you to fly from London to Athens?
   _____

2 We had to walk for an hour to reach the garage.
   It took us an hour for walk to the garage.
   _____

3 Phil did nothing but complain during the flight.
   Phil took the whole flight complaining.
   _____

4 Intercity trains don't usually stop at this station.
   It's unusual for Intercity trains stop at this station.
   _____

5 Rebecca is always getting lost.
   Rebecca can't avoid to get lost all the time.
   _____

Unit 13

H Opinion and discussion
Circle the rewritten sentence which does not contain any mistakes.

1 I just can't wait for the new boat to arrive.
   a I'm really looking forward for the new boat arriving.
   b I'm really looking forward to the new boat arriving.

2 'You've damaged the car, George', said George's dad.
   a George's dad accused him for damaging the car.
   b George's dad accused him of damaging the car.

3 Michael thinks that he's a very careful driver.
   a Michael believes himself to be a very careful driver.
   b Michael believes that himself is a very careful driver.

Grammar focus

Decide if these statements are true or false. Write T for True or F for False on the lines.

1 The causative form is **have/get something done**. _____
2 We use **get** when we want to be more formal. _____
3 In the sentence '**Carl is having his car cleaned.**' Carl is the person who cleans the car. _____
4 With the causative, we always say who is doing the action. _____
5 The causative can be used for unwanted actions too, as in the sentence '**I had my bike stolen.**' _____

Each of these sentences in the causative form contains a mistake. Rewrite the words in bold so that the sentence is correct.

1 Wendy **has** her car **cleaning** every two weeks.   present simple

2 We **getting** the plane tickets **delivered**.   present continuous

3 Gloria **has have** her skateboard **stolen**.   present perfect simple

4 I **get** my motorbike **fitted** with a more powerful engine.   past simple

5 Sam **was having** her car **repairing** when we gave her a lift.   past continuous

6 He **had** only **has** his boat **painted** a week before the accident.   past perfect simple

7 I hope they **will having** those cars **towed** away.   future simple

8 They **are going to have** the Rolls Royce **polish** again.   'going to'

9 I wonder if he **will had** the car **pulled** out of the lake.   future perfect

10 I had the bike repaired **from** a professional mechanic.   agent

11 We had the leather seats washed **by** a special detergent.   instrument

Exam practice — Use of English Part 3

Exam know-how

When you do Use of English Part 3:
- Think very carefully about patterns. A lot of the questions are testing if you know, for example, that it is 'manage to do something' but 'succeed in doing something'. Make sure you learn as many patterns as you can.
- Always make a guess if you are not sure. Each question is worth two marks, so it's possible to get one mark even if you don't get everything right. If you don't write anything, you will definitely get no marks!

For questions **1-10**, complete the second sentence so that it has a similar meaning to the first sentence, using the word given. **Do not change the word given**. You must use between **two** and **five** words, including the word given.

1. We didn't manage to get to Chicago by midnight.
   succeed
   We .... to Chicago by midnight.

2. Karen had difficulty carrying all the suitcases.
   difficult
   Karen .... all the suitcases.

3. 'Can you meet me at the station at three o'clock, John?' asked Phil.
   could
   Phil wanted to know .... at the station at three o'clock.

4. Greg definitely won't make it to the wedding now.
   chance
   Greg .... it to the wedding now.

5. It's their duty to carry the luggage to the cabins.
   responsible
   They .... the luggage to the cabins.

6. The Wilsons didn't want to do any more driving that night.
   feel
   The Wilsons .... any more driving that night.

7. Martin would really like to be able to water-ski.
   regrets
   Martin .... able to water-ski.

8. Elizabeth's parents didn't let her sit in the front.
   made
   Elizabeth .... in the back.

9. It's a waste of time for you to come all the way to the airport.
   worth
   It .... all the way to the airport.

10. I can't wait to go in the submarine.
    forward
    I'm really .... in the submarine.

Unit 14 Fashion

WARM-UP

Look at the picture.
In pairs, ask and answer the following questions:
- Do you enjoy shopping for clothes?
- Where do you usually buy clothes from?
- Do you prefer to go shopping for clothes on your own, with friends, or with family? Why?

DEVELOP YOUR USE OF ENGLISH SKILLS

A Conditionals

Circle the correct option(s) to fill each gap. There may be more than one correct option for each gap.

1 If you _____ go to the town centre, could you get me some socks?
  a will   **b** no word   **c** do

2 You can borrow my T-shirt, if you _____ like.
  a will   **b** no word   **c** do

3 If it _____ shrink a little, try gently stretching it.
  a should   **b** no word   **c** does

4 I'm not going shopping unless you _____ come too.
  a will   **b** no word   **c** have

5 Would you mind if I _____ got the same style jacket as you?
  a would   **b** no word   **c** did

6 I _____ try on a larger one, if I were you.
  a would   **b** no word   **c** did

7 If you _____ told me you were going to a fashion show, I'd have come with you.
  a had   **b** no word   **c** are

8 He would have _____ able to exchange it if he'd kept his receipt.
  a had   **b** no word   **c** been

B Auxiliary verbs and modals

One sentence in each of these pairs of sentences is correct. The other contains an extra word. Tick (✓) the correct sentences and circle the incorrect word in the other sentences.

1. a The fashion show will be ~~continue~~ after a short break. _____
   b Do you think she will be successful as a model? _____

2. a It would ~~seems~~ to me that modelling is rather boring. _____
   b It would seem to me to be a rather boring job. _____

3. a Sally had never ~~been~~ intended to spend so much on clothes. _____
   b Sally had never been given so much money before. _____

4. a I'd forgotten that you haven't got a swimming costume. _____
   b I'd forgotten that you don't ~~have~~ got a swimming costume. _____

5. a I took back the sweater which I had bought the week before. _____
   b Thanks for the sweater which you ~~had~~ sent me last week. _____

6. a Gucali's collection was ~~being~~ a big disappointment. _____
   b Gucali's son was being very silly. _____

7. a The shop had been closed for several months. _____
   b The shop was ~~been~~ closed when we got there. _____

8. a We had just ~~been~~ being served when the fire alarm went off. _____
   b We were just being served when the fire alarm went off. _____

9. a The models were all being photographed when I arrived. _____
   b The models were all ~~being~~ exhausted when I arrived. _____

10. a As you can ~~know~~, sports gear can be very expensive. _____
    b As you can see, sports gear can be very expensive. _____

11. a I did eventually find one in my size. _____
    b I did eventually ~~found~~ one in my size. _____

12. a You ought to try it on before you buy it. _____
    b You should ~~to~~ try it on before you buy it. _____

13. a It's more comfortable than ones I have bought in the past. _____
    b It's more comfortable than I ~~have~~ thought it would be. _____

Unit 14

DEVELOP YOUR USE OF ENGLISH SKILLS

 Relative clauses

Circle the correct word to complete these sentences. If no word is required, circle the dash (–).

1 Martin is the person who / – responsible for designing the team's sports kit.
2 The jeans are ideal for people who / – want to be both fashionable and comfortable.
3 I hadn't told anyone who / – I had had the photos taken at that stage.
4 My brother, who lives in England, he / – says that clothes are much cheaper there.
5 A friend of mine who / – has been a model for over four years.
6 The trainers, which they / – are made in Japan, are extremely popular in Germany.
7 The uniforms, which they / – have to buy when they join the school, are blue and white.
8 The skirt which / – was too small and I decided not to buy it.
9 The booklet tells you which are / – modelling agencies to avoid.
10 There are also knitting patterns which you can send off for them / –.
11 I found a tie that / – hidden at the back of the wardrobe.
12 Jenny's the girl I lent my leather jacket to / –.
13 Milan is the town where much of the Italian fashion industry is based there / –.

 Articles

Some of the articles ('a', 'an', 'the') in this passage are extra words which are incorrect. Find them, and circle them.

The Fashion Shoot

We're studying the fashion at the school at the moment, and the last week our teacher arranged for us to go on a trip to see a fashion shoot. It was the very exciting! We travelled by the coach to an old quarry which hasn't been used for the years, near a small village surrounded by the beautiful countryside. When we arrived, the photographer was just setting up his camera, and the models were putting on their make-up and generally getting ready. It was a fashion shoot for a mail-order clothing the catalogue. The weather was a lovely – perfect for the taking photos. We watched as the photographer told the models where to stand and how to pose. At the end of the shoot, which lasted the four hours, he took a photo of us, with the models. I've got a copy of it framed on my bedroom wall. Then, we talked to the models for a while, and they told us what a life was like working in the fashion an industry. It was all a very useful information for my course and I realised that they don't have an easy job to do. It was a very educational trip, and we all had a fun too.

E Time

Each of these sentences contains one extra word. Circle it and write it on the line at the end of the sentence.

1 Things went wrong as soon as I have got to the fancy dress party.   _____
2 I've had this dress for over than ten years and it still fits me.   _____
3 I'll do the ironing when I will get home from work.   _____
4 I'll help you with your make-up while I am being here, if you like.   _____
5 That clothes shop has been open for several years before now.   _____
6 Take as much time as you will need.   _____
7 We'll put this suit in the wardrobe until you will grow into it.   _____

F So, such and too

Some of these sentences can take 'so', 'such' or 'too' in the gap to complete them and some can't. Either write **so**, **such** or **too** to complete the sentence or put a dash (–) if it would be wrong to fill the gap with any of these words.

1 This is a _____ fantastic costume.
2 These are _____ cool trainers.
3 That suit's really _____ expensive for me to buy.
4 Super models _____ as Naomi Campbell earn an enormous amount of money.
5 Do you know how _____ much top models earn these days?
6 A new hairstyle can change your appearance _____ much.
7 Jacky thinks this jacket's really trendy, but I don't think _____.
8 I don't think _____ you'll find another pair of shoes like this.
9 Her earrings were _____ lovely.
10 It's _____ cheap I've just got to buy it.
11 I've never seen _____ a bright tie!
12 Skirts seem to be getting _____ shorter and shorter every year.
13 The sales were on _____ we decided to go clothes shopping.
14 I've never heard _____ nonsense. Of course red goes with green!
15 You can never have _____ many pairs of shoes.
16 Bella's got a new top so I want one _____.

G Adjectives, comparatives and superlatives

Circle the correct option to complete these sentences.

1 Getting a friend to trim your hair is more / – cheaper than going to a hairdresser.
2 It is much / more easier for women to become fashion models than men.
3 Trainers are more / – comfortable than high-heeled shoes.
4 I think the fashion industry is very much / – exciting.
5 These boots are more / rather big.
6 The rather / – biggest disadvantage of mail order is that you can't try the things on first.

Unit 14

H Amounts

Circle the correct word or phrase to fill each gap.

1. Debbie's had _____ different hairstyles.
   a lots   **b** lots of

2. My dad's got a _____ suits.
   a lot of   **b** lots of

3. This book doesn't have _____ information about dyeing clothes.
   a much   **b** many

4. How _____ pairs of jeans have you got?
   a much   **b** many

5. _____ models ever become really successful and famous.
   a A few   **b** Few

6. I've got _____ necklaces, but not that many.
   a a few   **b** few

7. I haven't got _____ money to buy that hat too.
   a enough of   **b** enough

8. Not everyone at the party was wearing a costume, but _____ people were, so it wasn't boring.
   a enough of   **b** enough

9. _____ my socks have got holes in them!
   a Some of   **b** Some

10. Sheila took _____ old clothes to the charity shop.
    a some of   **b** some

Grammar focus

First, decide if these sentences are grammatically correct or not. Put a tick (✓) or a cross (✗) on the first line.

When you have done that, for each correct sentence, think about whether it is referring to the past, now, generally, or the future. Write 'past', 'now', 'generally' or 'future' on the second line. You might need to write more than one time word on some of the lines.

1. I hope **to be a model** when I grow up. _____ _____
2. I hope **I win first prize** in the fashion competition. _____ _____
3. I hope I **haven't bought** the wrong size. _____ _____
4. I hope I **chose** the right style top for Jane. _____ _____
5. I hope these jeans **won't be too tight**. _____ _____
6. I hope Sheila **can come** to the fashion show tonight. _____ _____
7. I hope Angela **can sew**. _____ _____
8. I hope Adam **is coming shopping** with us. _____ _____
9. I wish I **am a famous designer** when I'm older. _____ _____
10. I wish I **could knit**. _____ _____
11. I wish you **could come shopping** with me. _____ _____
12. I wish hats **will come back** in fashion. _____ _____
13. I wish hats **would come back** in fashion. _____ _____
14. I wish I **was walking** down that catwalk. _____ _____
15. I wish I **had enough money** to buy those shoes. _____ _____
16. I wish I **hadn't spilt ink** all over this shirt. _____ _____

EXAM PRACTICE — USE OF ENGLISH PART 4

Exam know-how

When you do Use of English Part 4:
- Think very carefully about the grammar of each sentence. For every verb, ask yourself if it's in the right tense, or if an auxiliary verb or modal has been added to make it wrong. Be particularly careful with verbs in conditionals or coming after 'when', 'until', 'while' and 'as soon as'.
- Also pay careful attention to pronouns, relative pronouns and articles, and words like 'so', 'such', 'too', 'more', 'many', 'much', 'lots', 'rather'. These are often extra words.

For questions **1-15**, read the text below and look carefully at each line. Some of the lines are correct, and some have a word which should not be there. If a line is correct, put a tick (✓) by the number. If a line has a word which should **not** be there, write the word on the left. There are two examples at the beginning (**0** and **00**).

Examples:

0	being
00	✓

SECOND-HAND CLOTHES

0	being	When I was being a child, I used to hate second-hand clothes.
00	✓	I wanted all of my things to be new. I particularly hated it when
1		my mum she made me wear my older brother's school uniform.
2		I felt really silly and all the kids at a school laughed at me because
3		it was too big for me. Nowadays, however, things have been
4		changed. I don't like spending a lots of money on clothes, and
5		the fashion is for old-looking, second-hand clothes anyway, so I
6		get the most of my clothes from a charity shop. They have some
7		of fantastic stuff, and the money goes to charity too. The other day
8		I went to Oxfam – that's a famous charity shop in the UK – and
9		bought all sorts of things, which they were very fashionable, good
10		quality and extremely cheap. For example, I bought a denim
11		jacket, which I don't think so had ever been worn before, and
12		some more flared jeans. Flares are really in fashion at the moment.
13		I have also got a couple of very nice shirts there, and a white
14		T-shirt with which 'Young, Free and Single' written on it. All this
15		did cost less than twenty pounds. It's the best way to shop!

Practice Exam 7

Part 1

For questions **1-15**, read the text below and decide which answer (**A, B, C** or **D**) best fits each space. There is an example at the beginning (**0**).

Example:

| 0 | **A** given | **B** granted | **C** read | **D** said |

| 0 | A **B** C D |

CHEESE

Most of us take cheese for **(0)** .... When we go to the supermarket, we expect to see a **(1)** ..... of different cheeses to choose from. But have you ever wondered how these differences **(2)** ..... about?

Cheese has been produced and eaten for many thousands of years. No one knows for sure how we **(3)** ..... how to make cheese, but some animals, like lambs, produce cheese naturally in their stomachs. It's possible that our **(4)** ..... found this cheese-like **(5)** ..... in the stomach of a dead lamb or calf and liked the taste. Certainly, cheese is very practical. Milk **(6)** ..... very quickly, but turning it into a **(7)** ..... means that it can be kept for much longer. Cheese is also healthy, being full of protein, calcium and **(8)** ..... acids.

Cheese can be made from the milk of animals such as goats, sheep, cows, and **(9)** ..... horses and reindeer. By **(10)** ..... the most popular cheese in the world is Cheddar, an English cheese made from cow's milk.

The amount of water and fat used in the production of cheese **(11)** ..... whether it is hard or soft. The flavour of cheese **(12)** ..... on the kind of bacteria used in the ripening process. All cheese has bacteria in it, but this is not **(13)** ..... to humans.

The holes in Swiss cheese are made by bacteria that **(14)** ..... a certain gas. Roquefort and other blue cheeses are blue because they have a mould in them. Once **(15)** ..... , this is quite safe to eat.

1	**A** sort	**B** range	**C** variation	**D** distribution
2	**A** take	**B** are	**C** go	**D** came
3	**A** discovered	**B** invented	**C** worked	**D** succeeded
4	**A** elders	**B** descendants	**C** ancestors	**D** peers
5	**A** sort	**B** material	**C** substance	**D** type
6	**A** goes off	**B** takes out	**C** takes in	**D** ends up
7	**A** figure	**B** form	**C** shape	**D** solid
8	**A** famous	**B** noteworthy	**C** essential	**D** significant
9	**A** still	**B** even	**C** yet	**D** too
10	**A** far	**B** long	**C** high	**D** deep
11	**A** determines	**B** means	**C** decides	**D** says
12	**A** derives	**B** results	**C** relies	**D** depends
13	**A** bad	**B** harmful	**C** destructive	**D** unhelpful
14	**A** set in	**B** make up	**C** give off	**D** hand out
15	**A** again	**B** more	**C** over	**D** up

Part 2

For questions **16-30**, read the text below and think of the word which best fits each space. Use only **one** word in each space. There is an example at the beginning (**0**).

Example: | 0 | can |

THE JUNGLE

We **(0)** ...can... all imagine an intrepid explorer, cutting his way **(16)** .... a thick jungle. But **(17)** .... exactly is a jungle, and where are the great jungles of the world?

One definition **(18)** .... jungle is 'an area of thick tangled plant growth at ground level.' But, as this could also refer **(19)** .... your garden when you haven't had time to cut the grass for a week **(20)** .... two, the term 'jungle' **(21)** .... generally reserved to describe dense rain forests in tropical regions. However, some large forests in subtropical or even warm temperate regions are sometimes described **(22)** .... jungles. The major jungles **(23)** .... found in Central and South America, Africa and South East Asia. **(24)** .... are also jungles in North Australia, and even parts of the USA, **(25)** .... as Florida.

(26) .... it is rarely as hot as in the desert, the temperature in the jungle is always warm. Jungles are also categorised by their heavy rainfall, their darkness at ground level – due **(27)** .... the inability of sunlight to break through the thick vegetation – **(28)** .... the wide variety of plant and animal species found in them.

As **(29)** .... been widely reported recently, the great jungles of the world are now facing their greatest danger: humans. Each year, somewhere **(30)** .... seven and twenty million hectares of jungle are destroyed.

Part 3

For questions **31-40**, complete the second sentence so that it has a similar meaning to the first sentence, using the word given. **Do not change the word given**. You must use between **two** and **five** words, including the word given. Here is an example (**0**).

Example:

0 You must do exactly what the manager tells you.
    carry
    You must ………………………………………… instructions exactly.

The gap can be filled by the words 'carry out the manager's' so you write:

0	carry out the manager's

---

31 People say that Mandarin Chinese is a very difficult language to learn.
    supposed
    Mandarin Chinese ………………………………………… a very difficult language to learn.

32 My boss doesn't like me to be late for work.
    approve
    My boss ………………………………………… being late for work.

33 I don't want to go away this weekend.
    rather
    I ………………………………………… go away this weekend.

34 It's over five years since I last saw Joe.
    seen
    I ………………………………………… over five years.

35 She wouldn't have been able to pass the test without your help.
    helped
    She wouldn't have been able to pass the test ………………………………………… her.

36 Dave's always found sailing very easy.
    good
    Dave's always ………………………………………… sailing.

37 I just can't wait until my birthday!
    forward
    I ………………………………………… my birthday!

38 Adam behaved so badly his teacher sent him out of the classroom.
    so
    Adam's ………………………………………… his teacher sent him out of the classroom.

39 Jill was offered the job but didn't accept it because of the salary.
    turned
    Jill was offered the job but she ………………………………………… because of the salary.

40 It was unfair that the Russian ice-skater was given such low marks.
    deserve
    The Russian ice-skater ………………………………………… given such low marks.

Part 4

For questions **41-55**, read the text below and look carefully at each line. Some of the lines are correct, and some have a word which should not be there. If a line is correct, put a tick (✓) by the number. If a line has a word which should **not** be there, write the word on the left. There are two examples at the beginning (**0** and **00**).

Examples:

0	✓
00	the

THE SCHOOL TRIP

0	✓	Our class recently went on a trip to Stratford-Upon-Avon, the
00	the	birthplace of the William Shakespeare. It was a very interesting
41		day out. The town itself is too beautiful, as it's on a river and
42		there are a lots of Elizabethan buildings still standing. Some of
43		them are over five hundred years old! We looked round two
44		buildings: the house where Shakespeare was being born, and
45		Anne Hathaway's Cottage. Hathaway was Shakespeare's wife,
46		but she often stayed in Stratford while he was doing working
47		in London. In the same evening, we saw a production of
48		Shakespeare's comedy 'All's Well That Ends Well' at the Royal
49		Shakespeare Theatre. It was an extremely funny, and it wasn't
50		as difficult to understand as I had thought it would be. It wasn't
51		boring at all. The cast which were excellent, and I recognised a
52		couple of the actors from plays on television. It made me to want
53		to be in the next one school play! In the coach on the way back
54		to school, we sang songs and told lots of jokes. It was great fun,
55		but we were all very tired and I think so most of us fell asleep.

Part 5

For questions **56-65**, read the text below. Use the word given in capitals at the end of each line to form a word that fits in the space in the same line. There is an example at the beginning (**0**).

Example: | 0 | famous |

THE VALUE OF COMMERCIALS

How many (0) ...*famous*... caramel-coloured soft drinks can you think of? Probably **FAME**
no more than two. Why, then, do they spend millions of pounds on (56) .... **ADVERTISE**
their products each year? Surely their (57) .... would still buy them without **CUSTOM**
the commercials? In fact, it is because there is so little (58) .... that they feel **COMPETE**
it is (59) .... to spend so much on promotion. They are not so much trying to **USE**
increase their market share as to keep it.
Commercials help to keep a product (60) .... , and this keeps people buying **FASHION**
it. If the actors in the commercials aren't wearing the (61) .... clothes, young **LATE**
people will think that the product isn't 'cool', and may make the (62) .... not **DECIDE**
to buy it any more. Commercials undoubtedly have a (63) .... effect on **POWER**
what people purchase. For many companies, they are an extremely (64) .... **VALUE**
way of getting their message to a (65) .... audience of consumers. **WORLD**

Unit 15 Crime

WARM-UP — Pairwork

Look at the picture.
In pairs, ask and answer the following questions:
- What different things are the police responsible for?
- Are the police generally respected in your country?
- Would you like to be a policeman/woman? Why/Why not?

DEVELOP YOUR USE OF ENGLISH SKILLS

A Distance, size and power

Circle the correct words to complete this table.

Adjective	Noun	Verb
long	longness / **length**	longen / **lengthen**
short	**shortness** / shorth	**shorten** / enshort
wide	wideth / **width**	**widen** / widthen
broad	**breadth** / broadth	**broaden** / breadthen
deep	deepth / **depth**	depen / **deepen**
large	**largeness** / largth	largen / **enlarge**
high	hight / **height**	**heighten** / highten
low	**lowness** / lowth	lowen / **lower**
strong	**strength** / strength	**strengthen** / strongen
weak	**weakness** / weakth	**weaken** / enweak

B Complete the sentences

Use each word in bold to form a new word which fills the gap in the sentence.

1 We had a pool in prison, and I'd always swim twenty or thirty _____ a day. It kept me in shape. **long**

2 Policemen must be at least 1.5 metres in _____. **high**

3 The government has _____ the proposals to include victims of non-violent crimes such as fraud. **broad**

4 The detective asked for the photo to be _____ so she could make out the blurred face more clearly. **large**

5   Police are searching the length and _____ of the country in an attempt to apprehend the criminals. **broad**

6   The doors and windows have all been _____. No prisoner can escape from here. **strong**

7   It was awful. The _____ of the cell was only about one metre. I felt so claustrophobic. **wide**

8   We're launching a campaign to _____ awareness about the increase in crime in the area. **high**

9   The _____ of your prison sentence could be reduced for good behaviour. **long**

10 I wanted to be a detective but I failed the entry test because of my fear of _____. **high**

11 Police divers recovered the stolen car from a _____ of thirty metres. **deep**

12 The escaped convict lost a lot of blood during the prison break, and probably doesn't have the _____ to get very far. **strong**

13 If the police chief _____ the search area further, then he'll probably bring in forces from other areas to help in the search. **wide**

C Irregular nouns from verbs

Complete this table by filling in the column on the right. Be very careful! All the nouns you have to write are irregular in some way.

Verb	Noun		Verb	Noun
attend	_____ / *attendance*		marry	_____
believe	_____		permit	_____ / *permit*
choose	_____		practise	_____
decide	_____		pretend	_____
defend	_____		prove	_____
describe	_____		save	_____
die	_____		see	_____
explain	_____		solve	_____
furnish	_____		succeed	_____
give	_____		think	_____
intend	_____		vary	_____ / _____
lose	_____			

D Irregular nouns from adjectives

Now complete this table. Once again, be careful!

Adjective	Noun		Adjective	Noun
able	_____		evident	_____
anxious	_____		true	_____

Use of English Skills / Unit 15

Unit 15

DEVELOP YOUR USE OF ENGLISH SKILLS

E Irregular adjectives from nouns
Fill in the irregular adjectives to complete this table.

Adjective	Noun
_____	benefit
_____	day
_____	humour
_____ / _____ / _____ / _____ / _____ / _____	horror
_____	prison
_____	science
_____ / _____ / _____ / _____	terror

F Complete the passage
Use the word in bold to form a new word to fill each gap in this passage.

Does prison work?

There are several generally accepted _____ (**believe**) about prison. Firstly, that prison is a social _____ (**defend**) against anti-social people. In short, it keeps us _____ (**save**). Secondly, that prison punishes wrongdoers through their _____ (**lose**) of freedom. Thirdly, that it teaches convicts the error of their ways, so that when they are released, they can enter back into _____ (**day**) life as law-abiding citizens.

However, there is growing _____ (**evident**) that prison is not always the best _____ (**solve**) to the problems of crime that we face. Several _____ (**science**) studies have shown that prison is not nearly as _____ (**benefit**) to society as we might imagine. There are several _____ (**explain**) for this.

The _____ (**terror**) conditions in most prisons mean that _____ (**prison**) criminals rarely receive a positive education. Rather, they spend their time inside with other _____ (**prison**) who teach them the tricks of their trade. Also, when they are released, it's very difficult for them to find a job, so they often feel that they have no _____ (**choose**) but to reoffend. It's the only thing they know. So the _____ (**true**) is that they are more likely to commit crimes again when they are released than if they hadn't been sent to prison in the first place.

As a society, we have to pay _____ (**attend**) to the results of these findings. In _____ (**practise**), we may be a lot _____ (**save**) if we give criminals the _____ (**able**) to gain the practical skills they need to get a job and live _____ (**succeed**), productive lives, rather than just locking them away. There is little _____ (**prove**) that prison works. Perhaps now is the time for us to take important _____ (**decide**) regarding our system of punishment. At the very least, we need to give it more _____ (**think**). It could be a matter of life and _____ (**die**).

G Irregular comparatives and superlatives
Complete the table. Then, check your answers by looking at the chart on page 42.

Adjective / determiner		Comparative adjective	Superlative adjective
good		_____	_____
bad		_____	_____
far		_____	_____
much / many		_____	_____
little (=not much)		_____	_____
Normal adjective	**Normal adverb**	**Comparative adverb**	**Superlative adverb**
good	_____	_____	_____
bad	_____	_____	_____

H Circle the correct word
Circle the correct word to complete these sentences.

1 <u>More / Most</u> of the people I know have never even thought of committing a crime.
2 There's a lot <u>less / least</u> violent crime in this area than there used to be.
3 You did very <u>good / well</u> to tell the truth.
4 People drive a lot <u>badly / worse</u> after they've had alcohol.
5 It's the <u>worst / worse</u> case of stealing I've ever seen at this school. You're expelled!
6 Do you think community service is the <u>better / best</u> punishment for this crime?
7 The <u>further / furthest</u> he goes, the more evidence he'll leave behind him. Don't worry! We'll catch him!
8 The <u>less / least</u> punishment you can expect to receive is a fine.

I Irregular verbs
Complete these sentences by changing the form of the verb in bold. Write one word in each gap.

1 'We will do everything to make sure the terrorists are _____ to justice,' said the politician. **bring**
2 _____ in large letters on the sign were the words: 'Keep out!'. **write**
3 Joshua _____ a hole in the garden and buried the diamonds. **dig**
4 The window was _____ by the burglar. **break**
5 Over a million pounds worth of jewellery was _____ in the robbery. **steal**
6 I wish I hadn't _____ to live a life of crime. **choose**
7 The kidnappers were _____ and their captive was _____ to be unharmed. **catch / find**
8 The man who _____ the getaway car was blond and had a moustache. **drive**

Unit 15

J People
Complete this table.

Abstract noun	Person
advice	_____ / _____
crime	_____
employment	_____ / _____
law	_____
relationship	_____ / _____
sailing	_____
science	_____
surgery	_____

Grammar focus

First, decide whether these nouns are usually countable or uncountable, or both. Write C, U or C/U next to each one.

advice	____	furniture	____
glass	____	information	____
luggage	____	news	____
sheep	____	travel	____
cake	____	fish	____
hair	____	knowledge	____
money	____	person	____
time	____	work	____

Now decide whether these statements about countable and uncountable nouns are true or false. Write T for True or F for False on the line.

1. We can use the word 'many' with both countable and uncountable nouns. ____
2. We can use 'much' with uncountable nouns. ____
3. We usually only use 'much' and 'many' in questions and sentences with a negative verb. ____
4. We only use 'lots of' or 'a lot of' with countable nouns. ____
5. We can use 'some' with both countable and uncountable nouns. ____
6. We can only use 'a few' with countable nouns. ____
7. With uncountable nouns, 'a little' means 'a small amount of'. ____
8. With countable nouns, 'a little' means 'a small'. ____
9. We can say 'a piece of information/advice/furniture/cake/news'. ____
10. We usually use 'a number of' with countable nouns. ____
11. We usually use 'an amount of' with countable nouns. ____
12. 'Glass', 'hair' and 'time' have the same meaning whether they are countable or uncountable. ____

EXAM PRACTICE — USE OF ENGLISH PART 5

Exam know-how

When you do Use of English Part 5:
- Remember that some of the words tested in this part are irregular. Before the exam, try to learn as many irregular verbs, comparatives, nouns, etc as you can.
- Remember that spelling is very important in this part. You are not allowed to make any spelling mistakes. If there is a choice of answer, e.g. 'relative/relation' or 'advisor/adviser', just write one of the words. Do not write both.

For questions **1-10**, read the text below. Use the word given in capitals at the end of each line to form a word that fits in the space in the same line. There is an example at the beginning (**0**).

Example: | 0 | criminal |

THE POLICE LINE-UP

The main role of the police in (0) ...criminal... investigations is to uncover	**CRIME**
(1) .... which will lead to a prosecution. Sometimes, this is in the	**EVIDENT**
form of a (2) .... of the culprit by an eye-witness. The police use	**DESCRIBE**
this (3) .... to track down a likely suspect, and then approach	**INFORM**
people who have a similar (4) .... They ask them to take part in a line-up.	**APPEAR**
The suspect and the other people line up in a room. The witness	
enters with a policeman, and usually the suspect's (5) .... The	**LAW**
witness must look (6) .... at each person and say who they saw	**CARE**
committing the crime. Their (7) .... is extremely important. If they	**CHOOSE**
don't pick out the suspect, he may well be given his (8) .... and the	**FREE**
police will have to start the investigation again. The best (9)	**ADVISE**
for potential witnesses is to always tell the (10) .... , and only	**TRUE**
choose someone if you are absolutely certain it was them you saw.	

Unit 16 Shopping

WARM-UP — Pairwork

Look at the picture.
In pairs, ask and answer the following questions:
- How many different means of payment are there?
- What are their advantages/disadvantages?
- Do you have a credit card? If not, would you like to have one?

DEVELOP YOUR USE OF ENGLISH SKILLS

A Confusable words and phrases

Choose the correct word from each word group to fill each gap. There is one word in each group you will not use.

> receipt   recipe   bill   prescription

1 There's a wonderful pasta _____ in this cookbook.

2 I want to take this video back to the shop because the quality's not very good but I can't find the _____.

3 The doctor's given me a _____ for some antibiotics. Can you take it to the chemist for me?

> audience   sightseers   viewers   spectators   witnesses   onlookers

1 The _____ cheered as the two tennis players came onto the court.

2 The police are trying to put together a description of the robbers and are asking for any _____ to come forward.

3 The _____ who had happened to be passing when the accident occurred stood around watching as the paramedics loaded the stretcher onto the ambulance.

4 And if any _____ watching at home would like to take part in a future show, please call the number at the bottom of your screen now.

5 Half of the _____ walked out of the play during the interval. It clearly wasn't a successful first night performance.

124

| fortune | wages | salary | profit |

1 The company made a _____ of over £35,000 last year.
2 When I worked in the newsagent's, we used to collect our _____ every Friday.
3 As a successful lawyer, she earns a _____ of about £60,000 a year.

| trip | excursion | voyage | cruise | tour |

1 We went on a luxury _____ around the Caribbean last summer. It was fantastic!
2 Dan's away on a business _____ for the next couple of days.
3 Before air travel, people had to cross the Atlantic by ship. The _____ used to take about two weeks.
4 We're going to take a _____ of the pyramids while we're in Egypt.

| passes | spends | takes | lasts | finds |

1 Ralph _____ so much time on the internet – we never see him anymore!
2 I don't know how Gloria _____ the time to have a full-time job and bring up the kids. She's amazing!
3 It _____ about four hours to fly from the UK to Cyprus.
4 The time _____ so quickly at the weekend. I can't believe it's Sunday evening already.

| got in | got back | came in | came to |

1 When Isabelle _____ the room we all shouted 'Surprise!'.
2 We _____ home really late last night.
3 Darren _____ Manchester last weekend but I didn't get the chance to see him.

| in | at | to |

1 As soon as we arrived _____ Paris, we got a taxi to the centre.
2 When we arrived _____ the hospital, we found out that Angela had already had the baby.

| lost | failed | missed |

1 I can't believe we _____ the plane. It's your fault for spending so long in the duty free shop.
2 I _____ my purse somewhere in the department store but unfortunately no one handed it in.

Unit 16

DEVELOP YOUR USE OF ENGLISH SKILLS

B Correct the mistakes

Each of the words or phrases in bold is incorrect. Rewrite them correctly on the lines provided.

1 If you **will go** _____ into town tomorrow, could you get me some razors?
2 If I won a million euros, I don't think it **will** _____ change my life.
3 If you **haven't** _____ bought that new CD player, we'd have enough money to go out this weekend.
4 It is the first time I **am ever buying** _____ something over the internet.
5 It **had been** _____ the first time he had used his credit card.
6 I **had** _____ rather pay by cheque, if you don't mind.
7 I'd rather **pay** _____ by cash, but I didn't have enough on me.
8 I'd rather you **buy** _____ me something cheap for my birthday – don't spend a lot of money!
9 I'd rather you **haven't** _____ got barbecue-flavoured crisps. You know I don't like them very much.
10 I wish I **didn't buy** _____ this top. It looks awful on me.
11 I wish I **will have** _____ enough money to buy a new TV.
12 I wish Emma **came** _____ shopping with me later today. She's got such great taste.
13 I wish _____ I can find a parking space in the supermarket car park.
14 I'll show you what I've bought when I **will see** _____ you.
15 It's high time supermarkets **start** _____ delivering to villages as well as towns.

C Complete the sentences

Write one word in each gap to complete the sentences.

1 I can't believe they accused me _____ shoplifting.
2 Sam's going to apply _____ the job of Customer Services Manager.
3 I can't choose _____ the blue one and the red one. What do you think?
4 Security tags prevent a lot of goods _____ being stolen.
5 He succeeded _____ increasing sales of the new product.
6 I'm going to complain _____ the appalling service. It's outrageous!
7 We apologise _____ any inconvenience, but the shop is closing in five minutes.
8 I don't approve _____ credit cards. They just encourage people to get into debt.

9 I'm interested _____ these video recorders. Could you tell me something about them?
10 I'm not very keen _____ shopping. It's a bit boring.
11 Mr Partridge is the person responsible _____ Customer Services.
12 Hamley's is regarded _____ one of the best toy shops in the world.
13 I'm a bit short _____ money. Could you lend me some?
14 I'm very fond _____ Jim, but he does buy me the silliest presents.
15 If there's any problem, bring it back and we'll replace it. You can rely _____ us, Madam.
16 I'm not very good _____ using the internet. Can you show me how to book these plane tickets on-line?
17 I wasn't able _____ get a refund as I'd stupidly lost the receipt.
18 My husband's not capable _____ doing even the simplest shopping. He always buys the wrong things.
19 Did you manage _____ find those books you wanted?
20 My neighbour was arrested _____ shoplifting. It's his court case next week.

Make them negative
Write a prefix on these words to make them negative.

1 _____ legal   2 _____ normal   3 _____ possible   4 _____ accurate
5 _____ comfortable   6 _____ advantage   7 _____ patient   8 _____ security

So, such, too and enough
Circle the correct word or phrase to complete these sentences.

1 I haven't got enough money / money enough to buy these today.
2 You're so old / old enough to go into town on your own. You don't need me to come with you.
3 You're too young / young enough to go into town on your own. I'll go with you.
4 It was such an expensive / such expensive a computer game that I had to save up for weeks for it.
5 It's so / such expensive that I don't think I'll get it.

Relative pronouns
Write the correct relative pronoun ('who', 'which', etc) in each gap to complete these sentences.

1 Do you remember the day _____ we went shopping in Cardiff and the car broke down?
2 That's the shop assistant _____ was really rude to me last week.
3 I want to go to the checkout _____ you pay by cash.
4 That's the guy _____ father owns the corner shop opposite our house.
5 I ended up getting a mobile phone _____ is Pay-As-You-Go.

Unit 16

G Complete the sentences

Complete each sentence using the key word given so that it means the same as the first sentence. You must use between two and five words, including the key word.

1 My parents didn't let me buy the new Eminem CD. **not**
   I _____ the new Eminem CD.

2 I was forced to go to the supermarket for my mum. **made**
   My mum _____ to the supermarket for her.

3 Louise had difficulty getting the new table in the car. **difficult**
   Louise _____ the new table in the car.

4 It is Nicola's duty to deal with customers' complaints. **responsibility**
   Nicola _____ with customers' complaints.

5 There's no way we can offer you a refund. **impossible**
   It's _____ you a refund.

H Write the nouns and verbs

Complete the table.

Adjective	Noun	Verb
long	_____	_____
wide	_____	_____
broad	_____	_____
high	_____	_____
deep	_____	_____
strong	_____	_____

I Find the extra words

There are two extra words in each of these sentences. Find them and circle them.

1 Despite of the cost involved, we've not decided to get a new kitchen.
2 I told to you not to buy up a new sofa until the sales.
3 Grant is used to be a shopaholic but he's got it under a control now.
4 There's not much of milk left so that I'll go and get some more.
5 I did saw a lots of bargains in the sales.
6 Dad gave to Kieran twenty pounds to buy for his mum something nice for Mother's Day.
7 Very a few people manage to avoid getting into a debt at some point.
8 It's a too lovely dress but I don't think it would suit to me.
9 I must to start thinking about buying for my Christmas presents.
10 That's the person who responsible for the dealing with refunds.

J Match

Match each sentence 1-8 with the sentence a-h that explains what it means.

1 Robert stopped to look in the shop window. ____
2 Rob stopped looking in the shop window. ____
3 Bobbie denied stealing the leather jacket. ____
4 Bob refused to steal the leather jacket. ____
5 Robbie remembered to pick up his cashpoint card. ____
6 Roberto remembered picking up his cashpoint card. ____
7 Bert went on looking for a Chinese-French dictionary. ____
8 Bertie went on to look for a Chinese-French dictionary. ____

a He said he didn't do it.
b He continued his search.
c He was sure that he had.
d He decided he'd seen enough.
e He was doing something else and then he started his search.
f He was walking and then he saw something he liked.
g He said he wouldn't do it.
h He did this before he left home because he knew he'd need it.

Grammar focus

Choose the correct word or phrase to complete these sentences with inversions.
Remember that, in inversions, the verb is in the question form even though it's not a question.

1 I love shopping and so <u>my mum does / does my mum</u>.
2 Jo won't buy anything else and nor <u>will you / won't you</u>. You've both spent too much already.
3 I've never bought anything over the internet and neither <u>has / does</u> my husband and we're not going to start now, thank you very much!
4 Under no circumstances <u>can goods be / goods can be</u> returned without a valid receipt.
5 No sooner <u>had I arrived / did I arrive</u> than <u>I realised / did I realise</u> <u>I had lost / had I lost</u> my wallet.
6 Hardly had Mrs Bishop got off the bus <u>than / when</u> she bumped into Jackie Thompson.
7 Only after four hours did I <u>find / found</u> the CD I was looking for.
8 Never <u>have I met / I have met</u> a more helpful shop assistant.
9 Not only <u>was it / it was</u> in a sale, but <u>did I also get / I also got</u> a discount for paying cash.
10 Scarcely <u>had / hadn't</u> we entered the department store when I realised I couldn't find Daryl anywhere. I was frantic with worry.

Practice Exam 8

Part 1

For questions **1-15**, read the text below and decide which answer (**A**, **B**, **C** or **D**) best fits each space. There is an example at the beginning (**0**).

Example:

0   **A** mentioned   **B** called   **C** known   **D** referred

0	A	B	C	D

CHESS

Chess, often **(0)** ….. to as the Royal Game, is the oldest of all **(1)** ….. games which do not contain an element of **(2)** ….. .

The origins of chess are uncertain, **(3)** ….. there are a number of legends regarding its invention. One story **(4)** ….. that it was King Solomon who invented chess, another that it was the Greek god Hermes, and yet another that the Chinese mandarin Han-Sing was **(5)** ….. for its creation. In fact, chess almost certainly **(6)** ….. in India in the sixth or seventh century AD. The game's **(7)** ….. then spread quickly through Persia (now **(8)** ….. as Iran) and from there came to Europe. The first documented **(9)** ….. to chess in literature is in a Persian romance which was written about 600 AD.

It is **(10)** ….. the word 'chess' comes from 'shah', the Persian word for 'king' and that 'checkmate', the game's winning **(11)** ….. , comes from the phrase 'shah mat', **(12)** ….. 'the king is dead'.

The rules and pieces used in the game have **(13)** ….. changes over the centuries. Modern chess **(14)** ….. much to the Spaniard Ruy Lopez de Segura, who in 1561 wrote the first book on how to play the game. In it, he introduced the **(15)** ….. of 'castling', which had not been part of the game until then.

1	**A** board	**B** table	**C** panel	**D** top
2	**A** chance	**B** opportunity	**C** possibility	**D** probability
3	**A** despite	**B** nevertheless	**C** although	**D** however
4	**A** reads	**B** tells	**C** says	**D** writes
5	**A** reliable	**B** responsible	**C** dependable	**D** trustworthy
6	**A** created	**B** discovered	**C** invented	**D** originated
7	**A** celebrity	**B** knowledge	**C** popularity	**D** notoriety
8	**A** called	**B** known	**C** referred	**D** stated
9	**A** reference	**B** mention	**C** appeal	**D** indication
10	**A** believed	**B** imagined	**C** held	**D** taken
11	**A** place	**B** stand	**C** go	**D** move
12	**A** representing	**B** suggesting	**C** intending	**D** meaning
13	**A** underdone	**B** undergone	**C** overseen	**D** overtaken
14	**A** borrows	**B** lends	**C** owes	**D** pays
15	**A** belief	**B** concept	**C** view	**D** faith

Part 2

For questions **16-30**, read the text below and think of the word which best fits each space. Use only **one** word in each space. There is an example at the beginning (**0**).

Example: | 0 | into |

TEENAGER

The word 'teenager' only came **(0)** ....into.... existence in the 1940s. Before that, young people in their teens were generally **(16)** .... as 'adolescents' or just 'young adults'. This change in terminology marked a cultural and social change. **(17)** .... the first time in the West, adolescents were asserting their independence and creating a culture for **(18)** .... They were **(19)** .... to do this because of their increased spending power, brought **(20)** .... by their parents' increasing disposable income.

Teenagers in the West today are generally expected to achieve several goals. Firstly, they are expected to separate to a **(21)** .... extent from their families, and start to lead independent lives. It is **(22)** .... uncommon in countries such as the UK for teenagers to leave home **(23)** .... the age of sixteen. Secondly, they are expected to develop a sense of their **(24)** .... identity as male or female. Thirdly, they are expected to **(25)** .... completed their basic education by the end of **(26)** .... teens, and to be thinking about and starting to find a way of **(27)** .... a living.

Teenagers are often thought to be rebellious. This is for several reasons. The physical and hormonal changes that **(28)** .... place as we reach maturity can lead to some frustration and confusion, often producing some emotional imbalance. Moreover, for the last fifty years or so, **(29)** .... have been rapid changes in social attitudes. These often create differences in opinion **(30)** .... teenagers and the older generation.

Part 3

For questions **31-40**, complete the second sentence so that it has a similar meaning to the first sentence, using the word given. **Do not change the word given.** You must use between **two** and **five** words, including the word given. Here is an example (**0**).

Example:

0 You must do exactly what the manager tells you.
carry
You must .... instructions exactly.

The gap can be filled by the words 'carry out the manager's' so you write:

0	carry out the manager's

---

31 I am totally convinced that you'll pass the exam.
chance
In my opinion, there .... your failing the exam.

32 Not many people came to the wedding.
number
Only .... people came to the wedding.

33 I haven't got any money left.
run
I .... money.

34 The play was shorter than we had expected.
last
The play didn't .... we had expected.

35 I couldn't concentrate fully because of the noise coming from the next room.
hard
The noise coming from the next room .... to concentrate fully.

36 The twins described their experience to me in detail.
description
The twins gave .... their experience.

37 You can go to the cinema but you must get a taxi home afterwards.
long
You can go to the cinema .... a taxi home afterwards.

38 The flooding led to the road being closed.
result
The road had to .... of the flooding.

39 That contestant didn't succeed in getting to the final round of the quiz show.
to
That contestant didn't .... to the final round of the quiz show.

40 Carol would rather not come to the beach with us today.
feel
Carol .... to the beach with us today.

Part 4

For questions **41-55**, read the text below and look carefully at each line. Some of the lines are correct, and some have a word which should not be there. If a line is correct, put a tick (✓) by the number. If a line has a word which should **not** be there, write the word on the left. There are two examples at the beginning (**0** and **00**).

Examples: | 0 | ✓ | | 00 | of |

THE QUIZ SHOW

0	✓	My best friend Jenny appeared on a television quiz show a few
00	of	of nights ago. It was very exciting. We all knew that she would be
41		on, so all our friends met at her parents' house so to watch it.
42		Her parents videoed it too, of course. The programme was
43		started at half of past seven. We screamed and clapped when
44		we saw Jenny. She looked great. She had had her hair has
45		done, and was wearing the new top she had bought the day
46		before. She sat in the chair in the middle of the studio while the
47		presenter asked her some of questions. The questions got
48		harder and harder as they had increased in value. If she didn't
49		make any mistakes and got up the most difficult question right,
50		she would win a million pounds. By this time, Jenny had won a
51		thousand pounds. That was definitely for hers, whatever
52		happened. She answered to the next question correctly, which
53		was worth five thousand pounds. I didn't know the answer, but
54		she did know! Then, with the next question, she took a risk
55		but got the answer wrong. She was gone out of the game. Still, she had her thousand pounds, and we were very proud of her!

Part 5

For questions **56-65**, read the text below. Use the word given in capitals at the end of each line to form a word that fits in the space in the same line. There is an example at the beginning (**0**).

Example: | 0 | popularity |

A NEW GENERATION OF MOBILE PHONES?

Mobile phones have increased in (0) ...popularity... over the last few years, and these **POPULAR**
days almost everyone has one. We (56) .... use them mainly to make calls **CURRENT**
and to send text messages. Soon, however, (57) .... such as exactly where **INFORM**
you are, to the (58) .... few metres, may be available through a mobile. This **NEAR**
could be extremely (59) .... if you got lost, say when driving a car. There is **USE**
now no (60) .... reason why your phone shouldn't also be able to tell you **SCIENCE**
that you are entering an area of high (61) .... activity. Such technology has **CRIME**
been available to (62) .... such as the police and pilots for a long time, but **SPECIAL**
now that the (63) .... costs of such equipment have come down, mobile **FINANCE**
phone companies are looking at the (64) .... of offering these services to the **SUITABLE**
public. In their (65) .... , there will be a great demand for such services. It **JUDGE**
remains to be seen, of course, whether the public agrees.

Exam know-how

Remember that you only have 1 hour 30 minutes for all five Use of English parts. That means about 15 minutes for each part and 15 minutes to check all your answers.

How to do ... Use of English part 1

1 Read the instructions first to remind yourself what Part 1 of the exam involves.
2 Read through the whole text quickly to get a general idea of what the passage is about.
3 Look at the words you have been given for the first gap.
4 Try each word in the gap and read the sentence.
5 Sometimes the right answer depends on the meaning of the words you have been given and sometimes on the grammar of the sentence. Think about both.
6 If you are sure of the answer, make a note of it.
7 If you are not sure, cross off any answers you think are definitely wrong. Go on to the next gap.
8 When you reach the end, go back and look again at the ones you weren't sure about.
9 If you really can't decide between two or three of the words, make an EDUCATED GUESS. Don't leave any answers blank.
10 Quickly read through the whole passage again, trying your answers in the gaps to check them.
11 Carefully mark your answers on the separate answer sheet.

How to do ... Use of English part 2

1 Read the instructions first to remind yourself what Part 2 of the exam involves.
2 Read through the whole text quickly to get a general idea of what the passage is about.
3 As you read the text the first time, some of the answers may come to you. Make a note of them.
4 Look at the first gap. Read the whole sentence, paying particular attention to the words on either side of the gap.
5 Remember that the missing words are often auxiliary verbs, prepositions, pronouns, articles and other similar words.
6 There may be more than one answer for a gap. You, though, should choose only ONE word to fill each gap.
7 If you are sure of the answer, make a note of it.
8 If you are not sure, go on to the next gap.
9 When you reach the end, go back and look again at the ones you weren't sure about.
10 If you really aren't sure of the answer, make an EDUCATED GUESS. Don't leave any answers blank.
11 Quickly read through the whole passage again with your answers in the gaps. Does it sound right?
12 Carefully write your answers on the separate answer sheet. Write only ONE word in each box.

How to do ... Use of English part 3

1 Read the instructions first to remind yourself what Part 3 of the exam involves.
2 Read the first sentence.
3 Look at the word you have been given. What do you remember about the word? Is it followed by the gerund? Does it look like it might be part of a phrasal verb? Do you remember any phrases it appears in?
4 Look at the sentence you have been given to complete. Read the words you have been given.
5 Try to complete the gap using the word you have been given. Do not change the word given.
6 Remember that you should use between two and five words, including the word given. Contractions count as the number of words they would be if they weren't contracted, so 'don't' (do not) is two words and 'can't' (cannot) is one word.
7 Read your new sentence and the first sentence again. Does your sentence mean the same as the first?
8 Check you haven't missed any small words like 'it' or 'his' or 'that'.
9 Do the other questions in the same way.
10 Quickly read through your answers to check that you haven't missed any information from the sentences you have been given. Check your spelling.
11 Carefully write your answers on the separate answer sheet. Do not write the whole sentence. You only need to write the words that are missing.

HOW TO DO ... USE OF ENGLISH PART 4

1 Read the instructions first to remind yourself what Part 4 of the exam involves.
2 Read through the whole text quickly to get a general idea of what the passage is about.
3 DO NOT think about the lines yet. Think about the sentences.
4 Read the first sentence. Apart from the example, look for words in the sentence that shouldn't be there.
5 Remember that the extra words are often prepositions, pronouns, modal verbs, 'to', 'of', 'as', 'so' and other similar words.
6 Remember that a word might look right but be wrong because of something much later in the sentence, even on the next line. Read the WHOLE sentence.
7 When you think you have found an extra word, try reading the whole sentence without the word. Does it sound better?
8 Do the same with each sentence in the passage. A sentence might have more than one mistake in it.
9 When you have looked at all the sentences, look at the lines. If you have chosen two words in a line, look at the sentence again. Each line can only have ONE extra word.
10 Count the number of lines which don't have a mistake in them. There are usually between three and five lines which are correct. If you have a lot of correct lines, look at the sentences again and check for extra words.
11 Carefully write your answers on the separate answer sheet. Put a tick for those lines which are correct and write the extra word for those lines which are not correct.

HOW TO DO ... USE OF ENGLISH PART 5

1 Read the instructions first to remind yourself what Part 5 of the exam involves.
2 Read through the whole text quickly to get a general idea of what the passage is about.
3 Look at the first gap and decide what kind of word is needed (verb, noun, adjective, adverb).
4 Look at the word you have been given. Remember that you may need to change the word a lot or you may need to add a prefix (at the beginning) or a suffix (at the end).
5 Think about which form of the word you need. Remember that some words form more than one noun, adjective, etc, so you may need to think about the differences between the choices.
6 Check carefully whether the word you need should be negative. Read the whole sentence and think about the general meaning of the passage. The most common negative prefixes are 'un-' and 'in-'.
7 Check carefully whether the word you need should be plural.
8 Do the same with the remaining gaps.
9 Quickly read the whole passage again and check your answers. Ask yourself if any of them should be negative or plural.
10 Check your spelling carefully. Remember that you often have to change the spelling slightly when forming the missing words, e.g. you have to change the 'y' in 'vary' to an 'i' in 'variety'.
11 Carefully write your answers on the separate answer sheet.

Key First Certificate collocations and patterns

A

ability have an ability (to do)

able be able to do

absent be absent from sth

accident have an accident; be (involved) in an accident; do sth by accident

according according to sb

account on account of; take into account; account for sth

accuse accuse sb of sth/doing

achieve achieve sth

addicted be addicted to sth

admire admire sb (for sth/doing)

advance in advance; advance to/towards a place

advantage take advantage of sth; have an advantage over sth; be at an advantage; be an advantage (of sth)

advise advise sb to do; advise sb on/about sth; advise (sb) against sth

affect affect sth

afraid be afraid of sth/doing; be afraid (that) + clause; be afraid to do

afternoon in the afternoon; this afternoon; tomorrow afternoon

agree agree with sth; agree on sth; agree to do

agreement come to/reach an agreement (on/about sth); be in agreement (on/about/with) sth

ahead go straight ahead; go ahead; be ahead of sth

allow allow sb to do; allow sth

alternative alternative medicine; find/be an alternative (to sth)

amount an amount of sth; in large/small/etc amounts; amount to

announce announce sth (to sb); announce (that) + clause

announcement make an announcement (about sth)

anxious be anxious about sth/doing

apologise apologise (to sb) for sth/doing

appear appear to be; it appears (that) + clause

apply apply for sth; apply in writing

appointment make/have/break an appointment

approval show/give (your) approval for sth

approve approve of sth/doing; approve sth

argue argue with sb; argue about sth/doing; argue (that) + clause

argument have an argument (with sb) (about sth/doing)

arrange arrange sth (with sb); arrange for sb to do

arrangement make/have an arrangement (with sb) (to do)

arrest arrest sb for sth/doing

arrive arrive in (a town or city); arrive at (a building, e.g. a station); arrive there

ask ask sb sth; ask sb to do sth (for you); ask about/for sth; ask if/whether + clause

associate associate sth with sth

attach attach sth to sth; be attached to sth

attack attack sth; an attack on sth; go on the attack; attack sb for sth/doing

attempt make an attempt (at sth/doing); attempt to do; in an attempt to do

attention pay attention to sth; attract (sb's) attention; draw (sb's) attention to sth

attractive be attractive (to sb)

average on average

avoid avoid sth/doing

aware be aware of sth

B
ban ban sb from sth/doing; ban sth

bath have/take a bath; run a bath (for sb)

because because + clause; because of sth/doing

bed make the/your bed; go to bed; be/stay/lie in bed; get out of bed

beg beg sb (for sth); beg sb to do

begin begin to do; begin by doing; begin sth

beginning in the beginning; at the beginning (of sth)

belief hold a belief

believe believe sth; believe in sth; believe (that) + clause; believe yourself to be sth

belong belong to sb; belong to a club/etc

benefit benefit from sth; a benefit of sth

best make the best of sth; do your best; be the best at sth/doing

bit a bit + adjective; a bit of sth

blame blame sth (on sth); blame sb for sth/doing; take the blame (for sth/doing); put the blame on sth; be to blame (for sth/doing)

boast boast of/about sth/doing (to sb)

borrow borrow sth (from sb)

bother (not) bother doing; be a bother to do; bother sb

bothered can't be bothered to do; be not bothered; be bothered by sth

bottom at/on the bottom (of sth)

bound be bound to do

break have/take a break; lunch break; tea break; commercial break; break sth

business be in business; go somewhere on business; a business trip

C
capable be capable of doing

care care for sth; care about sth/doing; take care of sth

careful be careful with/about/of sth

cause cause sth/sb to do sth; (be/find/look for/etc) the cause of sth

certain make/be certain (that) + clause

chance have/take/get a chance to do; have a chance of doing; be some/little/etc chance of (your) doing; the chances of (your) doing; take a chance (on sth)

charge charge sb with sth; charge sb (for sth/doing); charge an amount of money; take charge (of sth/doing); be in charge (of sth/doing)

choose choose between; choose to do

Christmas at Christmas; this/next/last Christmas; on Christmas Day

claim claim to do/be; claim (that) + clause; make a claim

clock around the clock

close be close to sth/doing; close sth

combination combination of; in combination with

comment comment on sth; make a comment (to sb) about sth

compete compete against/with sb; compete for sth; compete in sth

complain complain (to sb) (about sth/doing); complain of sth

complaint have/make a complaint (about sth); write a letter of complaint (to sb)

compliment compliment sb on sth; pay sb a compliment

concentrate concentrate on sth/doing

conclusion come to the conclusion; in conclusion

confuse confuse sth with sth; be confused about/by sth

congratulate congratulate sb on sth/doing

consider consider sth/doing; consider if/whether + clause; consider sb for sth; be considered strange/normal/etc (for sb to do)

continue continue sth/doing; continue to do; continue with sth

control be in control (of sth); take control (of sth); be under control; be under the control of sb; be out of control; lose control (of sth)

convince convince sb (of sth); convince sb to do; convince sb (that) + clause

cooking do the cooking

cope cope with sth

correspond correspond with sb

courage have the courage to do; it takes courage to do

covered be covered in/with sth

criticise criticise sb (for sth/doing)

D

damage do/cause damage (to sth)

danger be in danger; be out of danger

day off have/take a day off

debt be in debt (to sb)

decision make/take a decision (to do sth); come to/reach a decision (about sth)

demand demand sth; demand (that) + clause; be in demand; a demand for sth

deny deny sth/doing

depend depend on sth; depend on sb; be dependent on sth

describe describe sth as; describe sth to sb

description give a description of sth

despite despite sth/doing; despite the fact (that) + clause

differ differ from sth

difference make a difference; tell the difference (between); there's no/some/little/etc difference between

difficult be difficult to do; find sth difficult; find it difficult to do

difficulty have difficulty (in) doing

direction a change of direction; in the direction of sth; in this/that direction

discuss discuss sth/doing (with sb)

discussion have a discussion (with sb) about sth/doing

disguise in disguise; wear a disguise; disguise yourself

disguised be disguised as sth

do do sth (about sth); do your best; do your homework; do the ironing; do the housework; do the cooking; do the washing-up; do damage (to sth); do a job; do an exercise; do an experiment; do research; do some work; do sb a favour; do well/badly (at/in sth); sth does you good; do sth good/bad/stupid/etc; do good; do your duty

doubt have a/no/some/etc doubt about sth; have no doubt (that) + clause; there is no doubt (that) + clause; be in doubt (that) + clause; doubt if/whether + clause

dream have a dream (about sth/doing); dream about sth/doing; dream of doing

duty do your duty; a sense of duty; be on duty

E

Easter at Easter; this/next/last Easter

effect have an effect (on sth); take effect

effort make an effort; put effort into sth/doing

end in the end; at the end (of sth); come to an end

enjoy enjoy yourself; enjoy sth/doing

enough have enough of sth; have enough sth (to do); verb + adjective/adverb + enough (to do)

evening in the evening; this evening; tomorrow evening

exam take/do/have/pass/fail an exam; sit (for) an exam

except except (for) sth/doing

exercise do an exercise; do some exercise; get exercise

expense at your own expense; a business expense

experience have an experience; have/gain/get experience in/at sth/doing; experience sth; be experienced in/at sth/doing

experiment do an experiment; experiment with sth/doing

explain explain (that) + clause; explain sth (to sb)

F

fact in fact; the fact (of the matter) is (that) + clause; face the facts; be a fact (that) + clause

fail fail an exam/test/etc; fail to do

family have a family

famous be famous for sth/doing

fancy fancy sth/sb/doing

fashion be in fashion; be/go out of fashion; fashion model

fault be at fault; find fault with sth

favour do sb a favour; owe sb a favour; be in favour of

feed feed an animal/etc; feed on sth

fill fill sth (up); be filled with sth (note: be full of sth)

fit get/stay/keep/be fit

floor on the (ground/first/second/etc) floor

fond be fond of sth/doing

force force sb to do sth; force sb into sth/doing

forget forget to do; forget about sth/doing; forget doing; forget if/whether + clause

forgive forgive sb for sth/doing

fortune make/earn/win/have a fortune

free be free to do; be free from sth/doing; free sth (from sth/doing); free time

friends make/become/be/stay friends (with sb)

full be full of sth (note: be filled with sth)

fun be/have fun; make fun of sb

fuss make/cause a fuss (about sth/doing)

G

glance glance at sth; cast a glance at sth

glimpse glimpse sth; catch a glimpse of sth

go be your go; have a go; go shopping; go skiing; go on holiday

good do sb good; be good for sb; be good at sth/doing

guilty be guilty of sth/doing

H

hair cut/brush/wash your hair; have/get your hair cut; have/get a haircut; have a hair wash

happen sth happens; happen to do

happy be happy to do sth; be happy for sb (to do sth); be happy about sth/doing

have have to do; have sth to do; have a party; have a good time (doing); have a meal; have a plan; have an idea; have an interview; have an argument; have a lesson; have a family; have an effect (on sth); have a chance to do; have difficulty (in) doing

head off the top of your head; head for/towards a place; head over heels

health be in good/bad/poor/etc health

hear hear sth; hear about sth; hear from sb

height in height; afraid of heights

hold hold on (to sth); put sb on hold

holiday go/be on holiday; have/take a holiday

home make yourself at home; be/stay at home; go home; make your way home

homework do your homework; have homework (to do)

hope hope (that) + clause; hope to do; hope for sth

hour half an hour; a quarter of an hour; in an hour

housework do (the) housework

I
idea question an idea; have an idea

impossible be impossible (for sb) to do; find sth impossible; find it impossible to do

impression give sb the impression; do an impression of sb; have the impression; make an impression (on sb)

in case in case + clause; in case of sth

in spite of in spite of sth/doing; in spite of the fact (that) + clause

increase increase sth; an increase in sth; an increase of a certain amount/percentage

independent be independent of/from sth

influence influence sth; have/be an influence on sb

inform inform sb (that) + clause; inform sb about/of sth

inject inject sth (into sth)

injection have an injection (for/against) sth; give (sb) an injection

insist insist on sth/doing; insist (that) + clause

instead of instead of sth/doing

intend intend to do; intend doing

intention have the/no intention of doing

interest have/take/express an interest in sth/doing; be in your interest to do

interested be interested in sth/doing

internet on the internet; over the internet; surf the internet

introduction with the introduction of sth; an introduction to sth

invite invite sb (to sth); invite sb to do

involve involve sth/doing; be involved in sth/doing

ironing do the ironing

J
job do a job; have a job (to do); apply for a job; take/get a job

join join sth; join in (with) sth

joke joke about sth/doing; joke with sb; tell a joke

K
keen be keen to do; be keen on sth/doing

know know (about) sth/doing; know of sb; know how to do; be known as sth

L
lack lack sth; a lack of sth; be lacking in sth

lead lead to sth; lead to your doing

learn learn about sth/doing; have a lot to learn about sth/doing; learn how to do

least at least; at the very least; last but not least

left be left (somewhere); go/turn/etc left; on the left; on the left-hand side; in the left-hand corner; be left-handed

legal be legal (for sb to do)

lend lend sth to sb; lend sb sth

let let sb do sth; note: be let = be rented

like like sth/doing; like to do; be like sth/doing; be like sb (to do)

likely be likely to do; it is likely (that) + clause

listen listen to sth

live live in/at a place; live on sth; live for sth; live to be a certain age

long (for) as long as; (for) a long time; take a long time (to do); long to do; long for sth (to do)

look look at sth; look for sth; have/take a look at sth; look forward to sth/doing

love love sth/doing; love to do; love for sth/doing; be in love with sb

M

mad be mad about sth/doing; go/become mad

make make sb do; be made to do; make a complaint; make a decision; make a difference (to sth); make (sb) a drink; make a fortune; make a fuss (about sth/doing); make a meal; make a mess; make a mistake; make a noise; make a phone call; make a plan; make a suggestion; make an arrangement; make an effort; make friends with sb; make fun of sb; make money; make sense (to do); make sure (that) + clause; make the bed; make the best of sth; make up your mind

manage manage to do

mean mean to do; it/this means (that) + clause; it/this means sth/doing

medicine take medicine; prescribe medicine; practise/study medicine; the best medicine; alternative medicine

mention mention sth (to sb); mention (that) + clause

mess make a mess (of sth)

mind make up your mind; bear (sth) in mind; be in two minds about sth/doing; change your mind (about sth/doing); cross your mind; to my mind; mind if + clause

mistake make a mistake; be a mistake (to do); mistake sb for sb; do sth by mistake

money make/earn/win/save/have money; spend money (on sth/doing); be short of money

mood be in a good/bad mood; be in the right/wrong mood

morning in the morning; this morning; tomorrow morning

N

necessary be necessary (for sb) (to do)

need in need of; no need for; need to do; sth needs sth/doing

news be in the news; be on the news; hear the news

night all night; during the night; at night

nightmare have/be a nightmare

noise make/hear (a) noise

note make/take (a) note of sth; note sth (down)

notice notice sth; notice sb doing; take notice of sth; at short notice

O
object object to sth/doing

occasion on this/that occasion; on the occasion of sth

offer offer sb sth; offer sth (to sb); offer to do

opinion in my opinion; give/express your/an opinion (about sth/doing); hold/have an opinion (about sth/doing)

order be in order; put sth in order; in order to do; give an order (to sb) (to do)

P
part take part in sth/doing; be a part of sth; part with sth

party have/throw/give a party; go to a party; dinner/birthday/etc party

pass pass sth (over) to sb; pass an exam/test/etc; pass a building/etc

past in the past; walk/go/etc past sth

permission give sb permission to do; ask (sb) for permission to do; have permission to do; ask for/get permission (from sb) to do

persuade persuade sb to do; persuade sb (that) + clause; persuade sb of sth

phone call make/receive/get a phone call

photo(graph) have/take a photo (of sth)

pity take pity on sb; pity sb; feel pity for sb

place take place; in place of

plan make/follow a plan; plan sth; plan to do

play play a part/role in sth; play with sth; play sth; have a part/role to play in sth; be/act/star in a play

pleasant be pleasant to sb

pleasure take pleasure in sth/doing; gain pleasure from sth/doing

plenty plenty of sth; plenty more sth; plenty to do

point there's no point (in) doing; see sb's point; make a point (of doing); take sb's point (about sth/doing); see the point (in/of) doing sth

polite be polite to sb

popular be popular with/among sb

prefer prefer to do (rather than [to] do); prefer sth (rather than sth); prefer sth/doing (to sth/doing)

prepare prepare sb for sth; prepare to do; be prepared for sth

pretend pretend to do; pretend (that) + clause

prevent prevent sth; prevent sb from doing; prevent sth from happening/etc

profit make a profit; profit from sth/doing

promise promise to do sth; promise sb sth; the promise of sth; give/make sb a promise

proud be proud of sth/doing

purpose do sth on purpose

Q
qualify qualify as/in sth

question ask a question; question an idea; in question

quite quite a lot of; quite + adjective

R

rather rather (not) do sth; rather than; rather + adjective/adverb

reach reach (a town, city, building, other place)

reason a reason why + clause; reason with sb

refer refer to sth; refer sb to sth

refuse refuse to do sth; refuse sth

regard regard sb as (being) sth

regret regret (not) doing; regret sth; regret to tell/inform you

rely rely on sth

remember remember to do; remember sth/doing; remember (that) + clause

research carry out/do research (on/into sth)

respect respect sth; respect sb for sth/doing; have respect for sth

responsibility have/take (the) responsibility for sth/doing

responsible be responsible for sth/doing

result be a result of sth/doing; result in sth; result in (your) doing; result from sth/doing

route plan your/a route; take a route

S

save save sb from sth/doing; save money; save time

say say sth (to sb); say (that) + clause

seem seem to be; it seems (that) + clause

send send sb sth; send sth (to sb)

sense make sense (to do sth); make sense of sth

settle settle on/into/for sth

shape be/get/stay in shape; the shape of sth

shopping do the shopping; go shopping

short be short of sth

shower take/have a shower; a rain shower

side (on) the opposite side; (on) the far side; side with sb; be on the winning/losing side

sight catch/lose sight of sth; be in sight of sth; at first sight

sights see the sights

sightseeing go sightseeing

silence in silence

similar be similar to sth/doing

solution be/find a solution (to sth)

specialise specialise in sth/doing

speed at (high/full/etc) speed; a burst of speed; speed limit

spend spend money (on sth/doing); spend time doing; spend time on sth

spread spread sth; spread sth over sth; spread to a place

stare stare at sth

stop stop sth/doing; stop to do; stop sb from doing

study study sth; study for sth

succeed succeed in doing; succeed in/at sth

suffer suffer from sth

suggest suggest sth/doing (to sb); suggest (that) + clause

suggestion make a suggestion

suitable be suitable for sth/doing

sure make/be sure (that) + clause; make/be sure of sth; be sure to do

surprise by surprise; be surprised at/by sth

T
take take place; take a decision; take pity on sb; take pleasure in sth/doing; take care; take turns; take part (in sth); take sth into account; take advantage of sth; take a break (from sth/doing); take a day off; take a holiday; take a job; take a look at sth; take a shower/bath; take an exam; take a photo of sth; take sth to do; take time to do

talent have a talent (for sth/doing); be talented at sth/doing

tell tell sb sth; tell sb (that) + clause; tell sb about sth/doing; tell sb (not) to do; tell a joke/story/etc; tell the time

tend tend to do

tendency have a tendency to do

think think that; think of sth/doing; think about sth/doing

time on time; (just) in time; the whole time; it's (high) time; it's about time; take your time (doing); take (a long/some/etc) time to do sth; sth takes up your time; spend time doing; spend time on sth; at that time; at the right time; time passes (quickly/slowly/etc); for the first time; find time to do sth; make/find time for sth; for the time being; have a good/nice time (doing)

tired be tired of sth/doing

top at/on the top (of sth)

tour go on/take a tour round somewhere; tour a place

trend a trend in sth; follow/set a trend

trip business trip; school trip; go on a trip; take a trip (to a place)

try try to do; try sth/doing; try and do

turn turn (a)round/away; turn sth over; in turn; take turns; be your turn (to do)

U
unlikely be unlikely to do; it is unlikely (that) + clause

use use sth (for sth/doing); use sth to do; be useful for sth/doing; be useful to sb

used used to do; be/get used to sth/doing

V
view have/hold/take a view; be sb's view (that) + clause; in my view; in view of; look at /see the view; a view of sth; a view from sth

voice in a low/deep/high/etc voice

W
wait wait for sth (to do sth); wait and see

warn warn sb about/against sth/doing; warn sb of sth; warn sb not to do

washing-up do the washing-up

waste be a waste of time; waste your time; industrial/household waste

watch watch sth; watch (out) for sth; keep watch; wear a watch

way lose/make/find your way; in a way; on the way; go all the way (to sth)

weather weather forecast; be under the weather

week all (last/this/next) week

willing be willing to do

wonder wonder about sth/doing; wonder if/whether/why + clause

work do some work; go to work; be at work; work as sth; work for sb; work hard; be out of work

world all over the world; around the world; the whole world; in the world; world record

worry worry about sth/doing; be worried (that) + clause

worth be worth sth/doing

write write about sth/doing; write sth down; write sth (to sb); write sb sth

wrong do wrong; do the wrong thing; be wrong; be the wrong thing to do; go wrong; the wrong way up

Phrasalperfect Glossary of phrasal verbs

ask after to ask for news about someone

back down to stop asking for something, or stop saying that you will do something

back out to decide not to do something you agreed to do

bank on to depend on something happening or on someone doing something

bend down to move the top part of your body forwards and downwards

break down if a machine or vehicle breaks down, it stops working

break out if something bad such as a war or disease breaks out, it starts

break out to escape from a prison

bring forward to change the date or time of an event so that it happens earlier

bring in to introduce a new law or system

bring on to be the cause of something bad, especially an illness

bring out to produce a new product and start to sell it

bring up to look after a child until he or she becomes an adult

bring up to start discussing a subject

call off to decide to stop something that is planned or is already happening

carry on to continue doing something

catch on to become popular or fashionable

catch on to understand

chase after to follow someone or something quickly in order to catch them

close down to stop doing business or operating permanently

come (a)round if a regular event comes round, it happens again

come (a)round to to change your opinion or decision

come across to find something or meet someone by chance

come by to get something, especially something that is hard to get

come down with to become ill with a particular disease, usually one that is not serious

come forward to offer help or information

come into if you come into something, it becomes yours when someone dies

come off to succeed

come on to develop or make progress

come on to start to be broadcast

come round if something comes round, it is given or shown to every person in a particular place

come round to go to a place where someone is, especially their house, in order to visit them

come round/to to become conscious again after being unconscious

come up with to think of something such as an idea or a plan

cross out to draw an X or a line through writing because it is wrong or you have decided to write something else

cut down on to start doing less of something, especially because it is bad for your health

cut off to make a place difficult or impossible to enter, leave, or communicate with

cut off to stop the supply of something or stop something working

dawn on if something dawns on you, you realize it for the first time

die down if something dies down, it becomes much less noisy, powerful, or active

do away with to get rid of something

do up to repair, paint, and improve an old building, car, boat, etc

drop off to start to sleep

drop off to take someone to a place in a car, usually without getting out of the car yourself

drop out to leave something such as an activity, school, or competition before you have finished what you intended to do

drown out to prevent a sound from being heard by making a louder noise

fall for to believe that a trick or a joke is true

fall for to fall in love with someone

fall out to stop being friendly with someone because you have had a disagreement with them

fill in to add information such as your name or address in the empty spaces on an official document

flick through to turn the pages of a book, magazine, newspaper, etc very quickly looking at some of the pages for a very short time

get away to go somewhere different from where you live in order to have a rest or holiday

get back to return to a place

get by to have just enough of something such as money or knowledge so that you can do what you need to do

get down to make someone feel sad or lose hope

get on for be almost a particular time, number, age, etc

get on if people get on, they like each other and are friendly to each other

get on if someone is getting on, they are fairly old

get through to use or finish something

give away to show an emotion or quality that you are trying to hide

give off to produce something such as heat or a smell

give out to give something to several people

give up to stop doing something you do regularly

go down to be remembered by many people for having done something

go into to deal with something in detail

go off if food or drink goes off, it is no longer fresh

go off to explode or be fired

go off to stop liking someone or something

go on to continue happening or doing something as before

go on to do something after doing something else

go over to repeat a series of things or think about them again in order to understand them completely

grow on if something or someone grows on you, you start to like them more

hand down to give something valuable to your children or grand-children, usually when you die

hand in to give something to a person in authority

hand out to give things to different people in a group

keep on to continue doing something

leave out to not include someone or something

let down to make someone disappointed by not doing something they are expecting you to do

let off to give someone little or no punishment for something they did wrong

let off to make something such as a bomb explode

look after to take care of someone or something and make certain that they have everything they need

look down on to think that you are better or more important than someone else

look into to try to discover the facts about something such as a problem or crime

look out used for warning someone to be careful, especially because they are likely to have an accident

look up to to admire and respect someone

look up to try to find a particular piece of information by looking in a book or on a list, or by using a computer

make for to move towards a place

make off to escape with something, especially something stolen

make out to pretend that something is true

make out to see, hear, or understand someone or something with difficulty

make out to write all the necessary information on a document such as a cheque

make up for to provide something good, so that something bad seems less important

make up to become friendly with someone again after an argument

make up to invent a story, poem, etc

name after to give someone or something the same name as someone or something else

narrow down to reduce the number of possibilities or choices

pass away to die

pass out to suddenly become unconscious, for example because you are too hot

pick on to keep treating someone badly or unfairly, especially by criticising them

pick up to go and meet someone or something that you have arranged to take somewhere in a vehicle

pop in to go somewhere quickly or for a short time

pull in if a vehicle or driver pulls in somewhere, they stop there

pull out to stop being involved in an activity, event, or situation

pull through to manage to stay alive after you have been very ill or very badly injured

put by to save an amount of money so that you can buy or pay for something in the future

put down to criticise someone, especially when other people are present, in a way that makes them feel stupid

put down to if you put something down to a particular reason, you think it has happened for that reason

put down to kill an animal using a drug because it is very old, ill, or dangerous

put forward to suggest something or offer an idea, opinion, reason, etc, especially so that people can discuss it and make a decision

put off to delay doing something

put off to make someone not want to do something, or make someone not like someone or something

put on if you put on weight, you become fatter

put out to make something stop burning

put through if you put a person or call through, you connect someone to the person they want to speak to on the telephone

put to to match something (a name, a date, etc) with something else

put to to say something to someone in a particular way

run out of to use all of something and not have any left

run over to hit someone or something with a vehicle and drive over them

sail through to do something or deal with something very easily

see off to go somewhere such as a station or airport with someone in order to say goodbye to them

see through to make it possible for someone to continue to the end of something, especially something unpleasant or difficult

see through to recognise that something is not true and not be tricked by it

see to to deal with someone or something

set off to start a journey or start going in a particular direction

set out to explain, describe, or arrange something in a clear and detailed way, especially in writing

set out to start a journey

set out to start doing or working on something in order to achieve an aim

set to to start doing something in a determined or enthusiastic way

set up to start something such as a business, organisation, or institution

settle down to become calm after being upset, nervous, or excited, or to make someone do this

settle down to begin to live a quieter life by getting married or staying permanently in a place

show off to behave in a way that is intended to attract people's attention and make them admire you

stand in for to do someone else's job temporarily while they are not available to do it

stand out to be easy to see or notice because of being different

take aback if you are taken aback, you are shocked or surprised, especially by something someone says or does to you

take after to look or behave like an older relative

take down to write down information or a statement

take in to trick someone into believing something that is not true

take off if an aircraft takes off, it leaves the ground and starts flying

take off to become successful or popular very fast

take off to remove something, especially a piece of clothing

take on to accept some work or responsibility

take on to start to employ someone

take to to begin to like someone or something

take to to start doing something as a habit

take up to fill a particular amount of space or time

take up to start doing something regularly as a habit, job, or interest

tear down to destroy or remove a structure or part of a structure

think through to consider the facts about something in an organised and thorough way

throw away to get rid of something that you no longer want

try on to put on a piece of clothing in order to see how it looks and whether it fits

turn down to refuse to accept an offer or request

turn in go to bed at night

turn into to change or develop into something different

turn off to stop using a piece of equipment by pressing a button or moving a switch

turn out to develop in a particular way or have a particular result

turn over to turn a page in a book or a sheet of paper so that the other side is towards you

turn round to return the same way that you came instead of continuing on your journey

turn up to come somewhere unexpectedly or without making a firm arrangement

wear off if something such as a pain or emotion wears off, you gradually stop feeling it

Phrasal perfect 1

Read these sentences and then use the words in bold to complete the sentences below.

- I have to stop playing tennis because it **takes up** too much of my free time.
- Why don't you **take up** a hobby, like stamp-collecting?
- Sarah's parents **brought** her **up** in a very traditional way.
- When I see my boss, I'm going to **bring up** the subject of a pay rise.
- If you're not sure of the meaning, why don't you **look** it **up** in the dictionary?
- I've always **looked up to** my grandfather for all the things he's achieved in his life.
- The actor **turned down** the offer of five million dollars because he thought he could get more money.
- My dad has **come down with** the flu and he's really quite ill at the moment.
- I really don't like Jordan because he thinks he's better than everybody and **looks down on** them.
- This table was **handed down** to me by my grandfather before he died.

1. I tried to _____ it _____ when I was at the library, but I couldn't find it.
2. Mum isn't feeling too well. I think she might be starting to _____ something.
3. My parents always _____ me _____ to be polite to people and to help as much as I can.
4. I can't believe you _____ his offer of so much money to work for one day!
5. Being in the school choir is a lot of fun, but it _____ all my time.
6. My grandmother says that when she was a child she _____ people older than her more than teenagers today do.
7. Why did you have to _____ the fact that I lost my job when you know I find it so embarrassing?
8. My doctor suggested that I _____ a sport or join a gym.
9. My grandmother has _____ a lot of jewellery to my mum, and I'll get it eventually.
10. Mr Burns _____ his neighbours because they can't afford a car as new as his.

Phrasal perfect 2

Read these sentences and then use the words in bold to complete the sentences below.

- I really don't want to **go into** my problems just now. Let's talk about it later.
- When her uncle died, Jenny **came into** a huge amount of money.
- When the princess kissed the frog, he **turned into** a handsome prince.
- Police are planning to **look into** the recent increase in crime in the area.
- Be careful with that dynamite or it'll **go off** in your hands!
- I used to like George, but I'm really starting to **go off** him since he had his hair cut.
- Is this milk fresh? It smells like it's **gone off** to me.
- As the plane **took off**, Jodie looked down at her home city for one last time.
- If the new business **takes off**, this time next year we'll be millionaires, Rodney.
- I wish you would **take off** that ridiculous red nose and listen to me! This is serious!

1. We should increase our share of the market if the new product _____.
2. My dad says that somebody should _____ the business deals that the Prime Minister has made with big companies.
3. Have these eggs _____? How long have you had them in the fridge?
4. Life was much easier after I _____ my grandfather's fortune.
5. Come in and _____ your coat and warm yourself by the fire!
6. My brother _____ a really quiet person when he went away to the army.
7. Is there somewhere private we can talk? I don't want to _____ it in front of all these people.
8. Be careful the firework doesn't _____ before everybody is standing away from it.
9. Before we _____, the stewardess gave a safety demonstration.
10. The Beatles used to be my favourite group, but I'm beginning to _____ them.

Phrasalperfect 3

Read these sentences and then use the words in bold to complete the sentences below.

- I'd like you all to please **turn over** to the next page.
- Dad was driving down the road when he **ran over** a cat.
- Before we start the next unit, I'd like to **go over** what we did yesterday.
- I was relying on Mike to help me move house, but he **let** me **down** and didn't come.
- The policeman started to **take down** in his notebook what the witness said.
- Mum was in a bad mood, but I **put** it **down to** the fact that she was very tired.
- 'I wish you wouldn't criticise me and **put** me **down** in public,' Meg said to her husband.
- Our dog was old and ill so we asked the vet to **put** him **down** to stop him suffering.
- I'm tired of moving from town to town and I'd like to **settle down** in one place.
- 'Please **settle down** and be quiet and I'll give you your homework back.'

1 I'm afraid your cat is really rather ill and the best thing is to _____ her _____.
2 I don't think a teacher should ever _____ a student in class.
3 Apparently, the driver was drunk and _____ two people waiting for a bus.
4 If I could just _____ your personal details, we'll send your order to you today.
5 I nervously started to _____ the page, wondering what would happen next.
6 The police _____ the accident _____ the fact that the driver fell asleep.
7 John's late for our appointment. That's the second time he's _____ me _____ this week.
8 I wish the children would _____ and go to sleep up there.
9 My boss called me into her office to _____ my report.
10 All I want to do is _____ and have a family.

Phrasalperfect 4

Read these sentences and then use the words in bold to complete the sentences below.

- Mr Wilson's secretary **put** me **through** to him when I called.
- We **flicked through** a few magazines while we waited in the doctor's waiting room.
- We seem to **get through** about ten litres of milk a week in my family.
- My mum asked me to **turn off** the TV and help her prepare dinner.
- The wedding was planned for Saturday but they've **put** it **off** until next Thursday.
- Blue cheese is liked by a lot of people but the smell always **puts** me **off**.
- Somebody **let off** a bomb in the centre of town and two people were injured.
- The police **let** me **off** with a warning when they found me in the old house.
- The effects of the aspirin eventually **wore off** and my headache returned.
- If my plan **comes off**, we could make a lot of money out of it.

1 Don't _____ those fireworks in here! Take them outside!
2 I hope my fancy dress party _____ and everybody has a good time.
3 'I'll _____ you _____ this time,' Mr Smith said, 'but don't do it again.'
4 I started to feel ill in the night, once the medicine I had taken _____.
5 Could you tell Angela that we've _____ the meeting _____ until Monday morning?
6 My dad is always complaining about the amount of chocolate my sister and I _____ in a week.
7 The receptionist _____ me _____ to the manager immediately but there was no answer.
8 I couldn't eat snails! Just the thought of where they live _____ me _____.
9 My mum _____ my school books to see if I'd done all my homework.
10 Could you pass me that remote control so that I can _____ the air conditioning?

Phrasalperfect 5

Read these sentences and then use the words in bold to complete the sentences below.

- I usually have to **look after** my baby nephew when his parents go out for the evening.
- Sean really **takes after** his dad. They're both mad about football.
- The policeman **chased after** the bank robber, but failed to catch him.
- Sandy **asked after** you when I bumped into her this morning. She said she hadn't seen you for ages.
- The Dawson Tower was **named after** its architect – Albert Edgar Dawson.
- I really need to **get away** for a few days. I'm under so much stress at work at the moment.
- Don't **throw** that **away**! It's made of glass, so it can be recycled.
- Guy said he wasn't nervous about giving the speech, but his shaking hands **gave** him **away**.
- The garage has decided to **do away with** petrol pump assistants. Drivers will have to fill up their own tanks.
- My great-great-grandfather **passed away** last night. It's very sad, but he was 106!

1 I'm going to _____ these old shoes. No one's ever going to wear them again, are they?
2 I'm afraid I've got some bad news. Your dog _____ in his sleep. I'm very sorry.
3 I've been asked to _____ my neighbour's cat for a fortnight when they go on holiday.
4 Our school's decided to _____ school uniforms. From next term, we can wear what we like.
5 Their house is called 'Woodstock'! It's _____ the music festival where they met in the 60s.
6 I hope Caroline _____ her grandmother. It'd be great to have another musician in the family.
7 Do you think you can _____ this weekend? We could hire a boat and go fishing.
8 I saw the woman drop her purse, so I picked it up, _____ her, and gave it back to her.
9 Rick said he was fine, but his tone of voice _____ how exhausted he was.
10 Mr Cross _____ you. He wondered if you were still planning to join the army.

Phrasalperfect 6

Read these sentences and then use the words in bold to complete the sentences below.

- It took the firemen four hours to **put** the fire **out**.
- If you make a mistake, just **cross** it **out**. Don't use correction fluid – it wastes too much time.
- The speech was **drowned out** by loud music coming from the next room. We couldn't hear a word she said!
- We've **run out of** milk. Shall I go and get some?
- We're planning to **bring out** our second album in the autumn. It'll be in the shops by Christmas.
- The invigilator **handed out** the exam papers and told the candidates they could begin.
- I finished the exam after half an hour, so I **handed in** my papers and went for a coffee!
- I'm really not feeling well enough to chair the meeting. Could you **stand in for** me, Clare?
- Hi Jan! I thought I'd just **pop in** and check everything's okay. I'll only stay five minutes.
- I know it's not a parking space but we can just **pull in** there for a minute, can't we?

1 I _____ over 400 leaflets in town this morning. People seemed very interested in the concert.
2 I can't print anything out as my printer's _____ ink.
3 Please _____ all cigarettes before entering the building.
4 I'm passing the chemist on my way home so I'll _____ and see if the photos are ready.
5 The politician was _____ by people shouting and yelling.
6 She _____ the application form last week, so she should hear whether she's got an interview soon.
7 Isabelle has asked Guy to _____ her while she's in Russia, so he'll be giving the lecture.
8 The company has decided to _____ a new magazine aimed at the teenage market.
9 We can't _____. We're on a motorway! You'll have to wait till we get to a service station.
10 I hated writing essays at school. I'd write something down and then _____ what I'd just written. It used to take me ages!

Phrasalperfect 7
Read these sentences and then use the words in bold to complete the sentences below.

- Unless we can **come up with** a solution by tomorrow, we're in real trouble.
- I couldn't believe it when Uncle Frank **turned up** on the doorstep after all these years!
- My dad made a fortune when he **set up** a business producing mobile phones.
- Of course it's true! You don't think I'd **make up** a story like that, do you?
- I'm sorry I said all those horrible things about you and I hope that we can **make up** and be friends again.
- But you agreed to play Cinderella in the school play months ago! You can't **pull out** now!
- If you are with somebody who **passes out**, loosen their clothes to make them comfortable.
- It's too dark. I can't really **make out** who's standing outside the door.
- I **made out** I was ill, even though I felt fine, so that my mum would let me have the day off school.
- Could you **make out** the cheque to 'A. Wilkins', please?

1 We're having a meeting to see if we can _____ some good ideas for the new school magazine.
2 Sometimes, Belinda _____ when she hasn't had anything to eat for a while.
3 Some countries have decided to _____ of the Olympics as a protest over the international situation.
4 Ed _____ that he was really rich at the party, but I know he doesn't have that much money.
5 When my aunt _____ this firm in 1950, it was much smaller than it is today.
6 By the time Simon _____, the party was almost over.
7 Can you _____ what that sign over there says?
8 Let's _____ and forget that silly argument.
9 When you _____ the cheque, don't forget to write the date.
10 I don't blame you for not believing Glen. He does _____ some dreadful lies sometimes.

Phrasalperfect 8
Read these sentences and then use the words in bold to complete the sentences below.

- Do you think war is going to **break out** in Africa?
- No prisoner has ever managed to **break out** of this prison.
- The Prime Minister had agreed to appear in a TV debate, but he **backed out** at the last minute.
- The course was so difficult that thirteen students **dropped out** before the end.
- We'd thought it might be a bit cold, but it **turned out** to be a lovely day.
- The company is planning to **take on** fifteen new employees next year.
- The pianist **went on** playing even though there was no one in the bar.
- She started by giving a history of the company, and then she **went on** to say what the company's vision was.
- My grandfather **is getting on** now – he must be in his mid-80s.
- Dave **gets on** well with everyone. He's very sociable and easy-going.

1 I _____ of university after the first term. I wasn't enjoying it at all.
2 I was worried Fiona wouldn't be able to keep up with us, but she _____ to be one of the strongest members of the team.
3 Ben _____ better with adults than children his own age. It's very strange!
4 We had to _____ a lot more staff to deal with the increasing demand. We'd no idea the product would be so successful.
5 Fighting between fans is expected to _____ when the two teams meet in Germany next week.
6 I had agreed to sign the contract with Thompson Limited, but I _____ when I discovered Fisher's were willing to offer more money.
7 Although my great-aunt _____, she still leads a very active life.
8 He started by looking at European literature, and then _____ to compare European and American novels.
9 No one knows how he managed to _____ of such a heavily guarded police cell.
10 The match _____ into extra time, with the winning goal being scored in the ninety-third minute.

Phrasalperfect 9

Read these sentences and then use the words in bold to complete the sentences below.

- Take your mobile phone with you just in case the car **breaks down** on the way and you need help.
- Jason is so tall that he has to **bend down** to get in through the front door.
- Many local shops have had to **close down** because of competition from supermarkets.
- If you've got a cough, you should try to **cut down on** the number of cigarettes you smoke.
- Our teacher waited for the noise to **die down** before she continued to speak.
- I can't eat seafood because it **brings on** an allergic reaction.
- I'm worried about your father; I think he's **taken on** too much at work and he looks very tired.
- I can't **carry on** having music lessons because I have a lot of work for school this year.
- Your English has really **come on** this year and you are almost ready for the exam.
- The film you wanted to see is on Channel 6, but it doesn't **come on** until nine thirty.

1 That documentary was supposed to _____ now, so why are they showing this comedy?
2 My dentist says I have to _____ the amount of sugar I eat, so no more sweets for me.
3 I think that's fixed the washing machine, but if it _____ again we'll have to get a new one.
4 The laughter began to _____ until the comedian told another hilarious joke.
5 Britain's smallest house is so tiny that you have to _____ when you are inside.
6 Don't you think you might have _____ too much with your schoolwork, the choir, volleyball practice and violin lessons?
7 Mark's reading hadn't _____ as much as his teacher had hoped, so he had a few extra lessons.
8 I wanted to _____ watching TV but my mum said I had to help with the washing up.
9 My grandfather has to avoid physical exercise and stress in case it _____ a heart attack.
10 The area has such bad economic problems that a lot of businesses have been forced to _____.

Phrasalperfect 10

Read these sentences and then use the words in bold to complete the sentences below.

- These flowers **give off** a horrible smell, like rotting meat, to attract flies.
- We all went to the airport to **see** Grandma **off** when she flew to America.
- If we want to be there by nine o'clock, we should **set off** two hours before.
- We don't make a lot of money, but we **get by** on what I earn at the shop.
- Every month, I try to **put** a little money **by** to save up for my holiday.
- The policeman asked me how I had **come by** the expensive watch.
- You need to **fill in** this form and then take it to the desk over there.
- The man **took** me **in** completely and I never even guessed that he wasn't a real policeman.
- The government is thinking of **bringing in** a law to ban gambling.
- I'm really tired, so I think I'm going to **turn in**. Goodnight, everyone.

1 You don't need to come to the station to _____ me _____. I'll be fine on my own.
2 They are _____ a longer break at school so that we have more time between lessons.
3 I don't know how we're going to _____ this month with all the bills we have to pay.
4 This cheese might _____ a strong smell, but it's actually delicious.
5 In court, the accused denied that he had _____ the money illegally.
6 I suggest you _____ some of your birthday money _____ until you decide what to buy.
7 It had been a long day on the beach and we were all ready to _____.
8 By wearing a workman's uniform, the thief _____ the old woman _____ and was invited into the house.
9 Do you think you could _____ this survey about supermarkets? It only takes five minutes.
10 We decided to _____ early the next day to avoid the rush hour traffic.

Phrasal perfect 11

Read these sentences and then use the words in bold to complete the sentences below.

- It's starting to rain. I suggest we **make for** that cave over there and shelter until it passes.
- My dad said he **fell for** my mum the very first time they met, at a party.
- You've got me by saying I've got ink on my face before. I'm not going to **fall for** that old trick again.
- My brother has had to **bring** the wedding **forward** from the 21st to the 16th.
- No witnesses to the murder have **come forward** and police are struggling to solve the crime.
- During the meeting, Mr Jones **put forward** a number of very interesting suggestions.
- Mrs Levington asked Iris to **give** the books **out** to the rest of the class while she wrote something on the board.
- I'm sorry I said what I did, but let's not **fall out** over such a small thing.
- Do exercises A and C for homework but **leave out** exercise B, please.
- I thought Simon was rich, so I was rather **taken aback** when he asked me to lend him some money.

1 I have to admit that I was a bit _____ when I first heard that I had won the essay competition.
2 Our art teacher told me to _____ brushes to all the pupils.
3 I suppose I _____ Kevin the first time we walked to school together.
4 We've been friends for ages, and I hope we don't _____, but there's something I have to say.
5 'I've listened to your lies for years,' Mrs Yates shouted at her husband, 'and I'm not going to _____ them this time.'
6 London? The best way from here is if you _____ Plymouth and then keep going in that direction.
7 The policeman warned me not to _____ anything _____ from my description of the accident.
8 According to reporters, two people have _____ and claim that they saw the crime take place.
9 I thought you _____ some good ideas when we were chatting to the boss this morning.
10 Do you think we could possibly _____ the meeting _____ to Monday, rather than Friday?

Phrasal perfect 12

Read these sentences and then use the words in bold to complete the sentences below.

- It's amazing how quickly the fashion for wearing flares **caught on.** No one was wearing them a year ago.
- I didn't ask the boss for a pay rise, but I think she **caught on** when I told her I'd spent this month's salary.
- Don't **bank on** Julian turning up on Saturday. He's not very reliable.
- No one can learn to ride a bike immediately. You've just got to **keep on** practising.
- Excuse me. Where's the changing room? I want to **try on** these jeans.
- The match had to be **called off** when hooligans invaded the pitch.
- We forgot to pay the bill and our electricity was **cut off**.
- The whole village was **cut off** for three days during the recent blizzard. We couldn't get anywhere!
- The robbers **made off** with over a million pounds worth of jewellery.
- I know you're the cleverest in the class, but there's no need to **show off** about it.

1 It might be hot enough to go to the beach tomorrow, but I wouldn't _____ it.
2 The island is totally _____ from the mainland in the winter. Ferries only run during the summer.
3 It was supposed to be a surprise party, but Sharon _____ when she saw me buying a cake.
4 The burglars _____ in a blue Fiat Bravo.
5 The event was _____ at the last minute due to poor ticket sales.
6 I like George, but I wish he wouldn't _____ all the time.
7 Environmental awareness really _____ in the 1980s. Suddenly, everyone was talking about being green.
8 If you're running a marathon, you've got to _____ going no matter how tired you get.
9 The water's going to be _____ for a few hours tomorrow while they repair the pipes.
10 I love your jacket! Can I _____ it _____?

Phrasalperfect 13

Read these sentences and then use the words in bold to complete the sentences below.

- Your teacher told me you've been **picking on** other children in the class. That's bullying and I won't stand for it!
- I **put on** so much weight on holiday. I'd better go on a diet.
- It's **getting on for** nine o'clock. They should be here soon.
- I didn't like that song when I first heard it, but it's **grown on** me. I quite like it now.
- John couldn't remember where he'd met her before, but then it **dawned on** him that he'd been introduced to her at a friend's wedding.
- She was so seriously ill that, at one point, the doctors weren't sure if she'd **pull through** or not.
- You can't quit now, Coach! You've got to **see** the team **through** to the end of the season.
- You don't fool me! I can **see through** your lies!
- We ought to **think through** this plan one more time. Maybe we've missed something important.
- Emma had thought the interview would be difficult, but she **sailed through** it and they offered her the job.

1. Robert De Niro _____ a huge amount of weight in order to play his latest role.
2. He says he's not in love with her, but I can _____ right _____ him. He's crazy about her!
3. Pete _____ the exam without making a single mistake. His last-minute revision had paid off.
4. I don't know why, but the boss has been _____ all of us lately. All he does is make rude comments.
5. I wouldn't have been able to _____ my illness without the support of my family.
6. I want to _____ things _____ very carefully before I decide about the job.
7. It's _____ half past eleven. We should be leaving soon.
8. It suddenly _____ me yesterday that I'd forgotten to send my mum a birthday card.
9. I wasn't sure I'd like living here, but it's really _____ me. It's actually a very nice place to live.
10. I have to _____ my students _____ to their exams before I can consider leaving.

Phrasalperfect 14

Read these sentences and then use the words in bold to complete the sentences below.

- 'Let me **put** it **to** you this way, Mrs Dawkins. I suspect you're not telling us the complete truth,' said the lawyer.
- I know her face, but I can't **put** a name **to** it.
- We had a lot of work to do, so we **set to** it as quickly as we could.
- I can't do all that paperwork tonight. I'll **see to** it in the morning.
- When I **came round/to** after my anaesthetic, I couldn't remember what I was doing in hospital.
- Tina and Harry are **coming round** this afternoon, so I'd better tidy up.
- I didn't want to go abroad this summer, but I'm **coming (a)round to** the idea now. It would be nice to get away.
- Spring is **coming (a)round** again, so now's the time to do those jobs in the garden you've been putting off.
- A letter's **come round** the office asking staff not to send personal e-mails during working hours.
- Once we realised we'd taken the wrong turning, we had to **turn round** and go back.

1. I know it happened in the nineteenth century, but I can't _____ an exact date _____ it.
2. Bill's parents are _____ for lunch on Sunday.
3. A soldier fainted on parade, and only _____ when someone threw some water over him.
4. I'm going to _____ it _____ Brian that either we get engaged or we split up.
5. We can't _____. We're on a motorway! We'll just have to drive in this direction for a while.
6. The new school year is _____ again soon, so it's time to think about getting all the kids' exercise books, pen sets and calculators.
7. A note from the Council has _____ reminding us to vote in the local elections next week.
8. We only had an hour to tidy up, so we all _____ and did as much as we could.
9. Let's not do the washing-up now. We can _____ it later, can't we?
10. Dave was furious when I first brought the dog home, but I think he's _____ it now.

Phrasalperfect 15

Read these sentences and then use the words in bold to complete the sentences below.

- There's one child in the class who **stands out** from all the rest; she's extremely good at languages.
- We didn't want to get stuck in traffic, so we **set out** at five in the morning.
- Bill Gates **set out** to create the largest software corporation in the world.
- Details of the proposed changes are **set out** in chapters three and four.
- **Look out!** There's a car coming!
- They're going to **tear down** the old cinema and build a car park.
- Cloudy, miserable days really **get** me **down**.
- Our neighbour threatened to take us to court, but he **backed down** when he realised he might not win.
- We've managed to **narrow** it **down** to only two or three options.
- He'll **go down** in history as one of the greatest Presidents ever.

1 After packing up the camp, they _____ on the steep climb up the mountain.
2 We've got a list of about 300 candidates, which we're going to _____ to ten.
3 He _____ to win the Nobel Prize for literature, but ended up writing for a Sunday newspaper.
4 No leader can ever be sure how they'll _____ in history.
5 Fiona Durrell _____ as being the best candidate by far. I think we should give her the job.
6 I'm not going to let their negative attitude _____ me _____. I've got to stay positive!
7 Locals have started to _____ the wall which, until recently, divided these two communities.
8 '_____,' I whispered. 'There's someone coming.'
9 The government had been planning to raise taxes, but they _____ following widespread protest.
10 Our findings are _____ in the following pages.

Phrasalperfect 16

Read these sentences and then use the words in bold to complete the sentences below.

- I **gave up** smoking about five years ago. It was the best decision I've ever made.
- I'm sorry I forgot your birthday. Can I take you out to dinner to **make up for** it?
- I'm going to take the car, so I'll **pick** you **up** outside your house at half past five, if you like.
- They're going to **do up** the old theatre and turn it into a multi-screen cinema complex.
- The kids don't usually walk to school. Phil **drops** them **off** on his way to work.
- I missed the end of the film. I was so tired I **dropped off** in front of the TV.
- Stan **came across** some old school photographs while he was clearing out the garden shed.
- I've **taken to** going for a run every morning before breakfast. It's not much fun, but I know it's good for me.
- Tim's really **taken to** DIY. He's not happy these days unless he's got a paint brush or a screwdriver in his hand.
- The traffic was dreadful, so we didn't **get back** until after midnight.

1 What time's the taxi coming to _____ Sean _____ tomorrow morning?
2 There isn't a bus stop there, but the driver usually _____ me _____ at the corner.
3 Don't wait up. We'll stop for something to eat on the way, so we'll _____ quite late.
4 My grandfather _____ eating red meat when he was sixty-five.
5 My dad's going to _____ the spare bedroom and he's asked me to do the wallpapering.
6 Andrea's _____ living here so quickly. You wouldn't believe she used to say she could never live in a village.
7 The kids were exhausted; they _____ as soon as their heads hit the pillow.
8 Nothing can _____ the years I spent in prison for a crime I didn't commit.
9 I _____ your phone number in an old address book so I thought I'd call to see how you're doing.
10 Stephen's _____ wearing a cowboy hat all the time – even at home. I hope it's just a phase!

UNIVERSITY of CAMBRIDGE
ESOL Examinations

Candidate Name
If not already printed, write name in CAPITALS and complete the Candidate No. grid (in pencil).

Candidate Signature

Examination Title

Centre

Supervisor:
If the candidate is ABSENT or has WITHDRAWN shade here ▭

Centre No.

Candidate No.

Examination Details

SAMPLE

Candidate Answer Sheet: FCE Paper 3 Use of English

Use a **PENCIL** (B or HB). Rub out any answer you wish to change with an eraser.

For **Part 1:** Mark ONE letter for each question. For example, if you think **C** is the right answer to the question, mark your answer sheet like this:

For **Parts 2, 3, 4** and **5:** Write your answers in the spaces next to the numbers like this:

Part 1					Part 2	Do not write here
1	A	B	C	D	16	1 16 0
2	A	B	C	D	17	1 17 0
3	A	B	C	D	18	1 18 0
4	A	B	C	D	19	1 19 0
5	A	B	C	D	20	1 20 0
6	A	B	C	D	21	1 21 0
7	A	B	C	D	22	1 22 0
8	A	B	C	D	23	1 23 0
9	A	B	C	D	24	1 24 0
10	A	B	C	D	25	1 25 0
11	A	B	C	D	26	1 26 0
12	A	B	C	D	27	1 27 0
13	A	B	C	D	28	1 28 0
14	A	B	C	D	29	1 29 0
15	A	B	C	D	30	1 30 0

Turn over for Parts 3 - 5 →

FCE 3   Reproduced by permission of the University of Cambridge Local Examinations Syndicate   DP319/093

Part 3

#		
31		0 1 2
32		0 1 2
33		0 1 2
34		0 1 2
35		0 1 2
36		0 1 2
37		0 1 2
38		0 1 2
39		0 1 2
40		0 1 2

Part 4

#	
41	
42	
43	
44	
45	
46	
47	
48	
49	
50	
51	
52	
53	
54	
55	

Part 5

#	
56	
57	
58	
59	
60	
61	
62	
63	
64	
65	

Reproduced by permission of the University of Cambridge Local Examinations Syndicate